JUN 1 9 2012

diamond in the rough

diamond in the rough

SHAWN COLVIN

wm

WILLIAM MORROW
An Imprint of HarperCollins*Publishers*

HarperCollins books may be purchased for educational, business, or sales promotional use. For information please write: Special Markets Department, HarperCollins Publishers, 10 East 53rd Street, New York, NY 10022.

FIRST EDITION

Designed by Diahann Sturge

Library of Congress Cataloging-in-Publication Data has been applied for.

ISBN 978-0-06-175959-8

12 13 14 15 16 OV/RRD 10 9 8 7 6 5 4 3 2 1

To Caledonia, Mimi, and Papa

Put your ear down close to your soul and listen hard.

—Anne Sexton

Contents

Prologue   1

1 Light the Sky   5

2 A Vengeance   21

3 She Opened a Book   33

4 Get the Kids   41

5 Small Repairs   49

6 Walking on a Wire   59

7 Out There on Her Own   67

8 Dry Is Good   73

9 Wind Is Better   83

10   Go On and Do It   89

11   A Mission   105

12   She's All Right   115

13   Days Go By   131

14   You Always Knew It   141

15   Sunny Came Home   149

16   Hold on Tight   161

17   A List of Names   175

18   Bring a Sweater   181

19   I'm Hypnotized   189

20   Out of My Mind   195

21   Her Favorite Room   203

     Epilogue   219

     Acknowledgments   223

Prologue

Who doesn't have a bit of pyromania in them? There's something thrilling about making fire—it's primal, right? As a kid in rural South Dakota, I remember wandering one day out onto a vast, grassy field wielding a pack of matches from my father's pipe drawer, with the express purpose of burning something. It seemed so inviting to light a fire or two. Almost as good as burning up an ant by letting the sun shine onto it through a magnifying glass. I made small piles of grass, set them ablaze, and stomped them out. Eventually, I couldn't resist making multiple piles and my tiny fires, with the help of some wind, suddenly turned into one big one. I stomped for all I was worth, but it was no use, I had me a *fire*, and I went running to the house to tell my father, swearing with big wide eyes that I'd just *found* it, I didn't know how it happened. He didn't believe me, of course, but as parents will do at times when they know you've just gone through a rite of passage, like saying the dog ate your homework, my dad let it go and extinguished the fire.

Having learned nothing from this experience, I went on as an adult to continue setting fires. It's true. Twice I've burned up memorabilia from relationships with fools who have broken up with me. One of them, a long-distance affair, quit me over the phone with the line, "I've got cats to feed." In all fairness, this very short-lived "relationship" was mostly an illusion on my part, born of the simple desire to have a boyfriend. I'd met him at a gig somewhere and was smitten immediately. Adorable in a totally nerdy way, he played this card to great effect by wearing glasses he didn't need, and I'm a sucker for that professorial–cum–Dennis the Menace look. He'd seen a video of mine and thought I had nice legs. Game on! He didn't know what he wanted, but I did. Okay, so he still lived with his parents. And he was younger than me. I wanted a boyfriend. My philosophy tends to be that in the absence of a genuine relationship I am only too happy to invent one. Didn't the simple desire to be with someone, in addition to mutual attraction, make it a fait accompli? Uh, no. There were literal and figurative miles between us, and try as I might, I could not make the thing fly.

In short order I wore him out by demanding attention he couldn't provide, and he needed to feed the cats, of course. I decided to lay it all to rest by incinerating whatever I could find that reminded me of him. There was virtually nothing to burn—a few photographs and a cashed check I'd written him so he could come see me once. I set out a small cookie tin on the living-room rug of my apartment and lit my funeral pyre.

Just like when I was a kid, there was trouble. My carpet was made of synthetic fibers, and when the heat hit it, it started to melt. The rug was new, a remnant I got cheap at ABC Carpet and Home (the holy grail of decor), the color of the Caribbean, which I felt was a strong choice, especially with my pumpkin velveteen sofa. Very Renaissance. In horror, I caught the unmistakable odor of burning plastic, and with some oven mitts picked up the blazing tin as my rug seared and bubbled. You'd think I'd have learned my lesson, but no.

The next time I set fire to keepsakes from a lover was fairly recently. He drifted from place to place, which was romantic but hardly practical. On top of this there were children (both of us), an ex-wife (his), two ex-husbands (delicate cough), and midlife crises and stalled careers (across the board). But in my never-say-die fashion, I hung on. By God, I wanted a boyfriend. I was entitled to a boyfriend. It's just as well if they live far away, because I can't live with anyone. Another subject altogether. Anyhow, two years down that ever-challenging long-distance road—and let's not forget I tour half the year as well—it was all over.

This having been a longer affair than that other one, I had plenty of things to burn up. Cards, letters, photos, locks of hair (not paper and stinky when burned, FYI). The jewelry I kept. Fortunate enough to have a fireplace this time, I was all set as far as the carpet problem went. The only remedy for my anguish was to torch the offending items. I tossed them into the fireplace, lit a match, and let the healing begin. Of course the flue was shut. Of course I couldn't open it, since I depend on boyfriends for things like that. The house started to fill up with smoke. It happened to be the morning of my daughter's eighth birthday, and we were going to have a party, so I frantically threw open all the windows and went running around trying to find fans. It was July, and later, at the party, no one could understand why the house smelled like Christmas.

All my fires backfired. But Sunny's didn't. Sunny is the arsonist in what is probably my best-known song, "Sunny Came Home," and I've been asked more than a few times what was she building in her kitchen with her tools, what did she set fire to, and why? First of all, Sunny is me. Everything I write is through me, through my perspective. That realization is what helped me write songs in the first place. There's nothing under the sun that hasn't been said before, but no one can say what I have to say except me. Both Sunny and I went through a lot, I suppose, and came out the other side (at least I like to think Sunny was acquitted). She may have gone overboard a tad, but we are both of us survivors. I think it's safe to say she was pretty pissed and burned the house down. Why? We may never know. But I may be able to offer some clues.

They gave me Dilaudid. They had to give me something. I was on a gurney in South Austin Hospital with a kidney stone, a broken heart, and an unrelenting, treatment-resistant depression. At least they had something for the kidney stone. Dilaudid, or pharmaceutical heroin. It was good stuff. One shot of it wasn't enough to kill the pain, so they gave me two. Being a recovering alcoholic and drug addict, I now understood with new clarity why it had been such a blessing that I'd never tried heroin. Not only did the Dilaudid take away the physical pain, it made me euphoric. What depression? What heartbreak? I was high, of course.

Still, I held on to the possibility that maybe the Dilaudid would allow me to turn a corner and launch me into a state of emotional well-being as if by magic. Like the old theory that hypothesized if one got hit on the head and developed amnesia, then perhaps another blow to the head would reverse it. Like the way we attempt to fix the television's lousy reception by banging our fist on top of it.

Maybe this last kick while I was down, after being dumped, after sinking into the black hole, maybe this would be my salvation. Maybe the agony from the kidney stone and the sweet relief of the Dilaudid were a metaphor for the absolute bottom of the pit I'd been in, maybe the Dilaudid would miraculously heal my heart, fill it up and over, nudge the neurotransmitters in my brain back into rhythm, jolt them out of their amnesia, make them remember how to work again, so that when I woke up the next day, my very being would be rebooted. Restored to its original settings.

1
Light the Sky

South Dakota, 1960

It's like ten miles of two-lane
On a South Dakota wheat plain.

I was born on the prairie, in southeastern South Dakota. If you want wide-open spaces to throw your imagination at, the Great Plains are the place to be. When I was ten, my father decided we should live out in the country (as opposed to Vermillion, our bustling town of six thousand back then), and I used to walk the fields out there for literally hours in my Beatle boots and my mother's black leather jacket and pretend I was a Beatle. I guess I see my life as pretty much starting when I heard the Beatles. It was in this house I listened to "Not a Second Time" over and over on my record player until my father begged me to stop. Even then I was sophisticated enough to go for the deep tracks.

I had a very, very best friend named Ruth Noble, and we were misfits together, considering ourselves a little superior in our quirkiness. We didn't care about dolls or horses; we liked puzzles and junior church choir and Mr. Wizard. Her older sister, Jane, was the keeper of the Beatles albums, so Ruth's house was better, but you couldn't just grab a record and play it. Permission was required, and often denied, and I always had one eye out for Jane and the possibility of listening to the Beatles. I just lived for it.

It wasn't as though we were immune to the pop-idol syndrome—those moptops were awfully cute. But it was the new sound that got to me. Up till then I had heard only church music and my parents' record collection, which consisted of things like the Kingston Trio, Pete Seeger, and sound tracks for *Porgy and Bess* and *The Sound of Music*. There was a novelty song called "Wolverton Mountain," which was just insipid and silly, and my folks played it to death. If we could get Top 40 radio, I didn't know about it. However, we did have television—and we watched Ed Sullivan. Enough said.

So, as a Beatle, I would tromp around the fields as if I owned them, and maybe I did. The plains coaxed my dreams and fantasies with their bleak nothingness. The unending earth and sky were like a blank canvas, inviting any idea to be outlined and filled in. And the storms of the Midwest are like nothing else. *The Wizard of Oz* had it right. You can watch them come in from far away, even see the clear definition of receding blue pushed up against gigantic blackness, and wait for the first wind as the dark clouds pass over, bringing wild rain and thunder and lightning. These storms frightened me as a kid, and I'll never forget my father, loving them as he did, taking us out on the porch during those fantastic midwestern tempests and telling us about the different storms he remembered, from his youth right up through being in the army. And so I began to love storms, too.

Vermillion was not a town of diversity. I saw only white people for eleven years. We went to school, went to church, rode bikes, and pretended. My daughter goes to theater troupe and therapy (a chip off the old block), while her friends go to soccer practice, voice lessons, and the Shambala Center, and summers consist of all manner of camps. There was none of that. We were not overscheduled, because there was nothing to do. We were not overprotected, because there was nothing to fear. We walked and biked to and from school and the pool and one another's houses and played tag until we were called in after dark. During the winter we stayed in or sledded down some pitiful hill or skated on the river. Our Main Street sported Jacobsen's Bakery, the Tip Top Café, and the Piggly Wiggly. To get to our house, you turned right at the bowling alley.

The two-hour drive to my grandmother's in Mount Vernon, South Dakota, which had one paved road, was the general extent of my travels for a very long time. On the way there, you could pass through Mitchell, home of the Corn Palace, also referred to as the world's largest bird feeder. This was as far out of Vermillion as I got. I honestly cannot remember the first time I saw an ocean, and the very first plane ride I took was when I was twelve and we were moving to London, Ontario, Canada.

A very big day could involve driving the thirty minutes to Sioux City, Iowa, where we might buy fabric or see a movie and eat at Bishop's Cafeteria, where I would be overwhelmed by the array of choices and breathless knowing that at the end of the line I would be allowed to get chocolate cream pie with shavings of chocolate on top, a rare delicacy.

We couldn't afford vacations, and my father adored the outdoors, so he purchased a pop-up camper trailer, which we would haul to various destinations and camp. One of our favorite places was Lewis and Clark Lake near Yankton, South Dakota, about half an hour from Vermillion. We'd swim all day and play cards by lantern at night, falling into exhausted, dreamless sleep in our beds, all of us cozily together in our little camper, waking up to crisp mornings of campfire bacon and eggs and toast.

Before my younger brother and sister were born, it was easier to take car trips. The four of us—my brother, myself, and Mom and Dad—made a number of journeys in our bronze Rambler. Of course, one of them had to have been to the Black Hills and Mount Rushmore and the Badlands of South Dakota in the western part of our state, a world away from flat Vermillion in the southeast corner. These car trips could've been long, arduous, and thankless exercises in getting from one place to the next, but my parents made them into fun and games for Geoff and me, and I remember them dearly.

When we were quite young, we were introduced to the car game called Zitz. I think my mother or father must've made it up—"Zitz" was code for "cows," and when one spotted cattle, one was to loudly cry, "Zitz!" It was a pretty ingenious game for little kids, since there was no shortage of cows in South Dakota. Eventually we graduated to the more sophisticated Stinky Pinky, a game that required actual thought. To play Stinky Pinky, you thought of an adjective and a noun that rhymed, hence the name "Stinky Pinky," and described the thing without rhyming in order to challenge the other players to guess your Stinky Pinky. You started out simply; a "farm animal's sea vessel" would naturally be a "goat boat," and so forth, although single-syllable answers were called "Stink Pinks," two-syllables "Stinky Pinkys," and of course three-syllable rhymes were "Stinkity Pinkitys." One of my father's favorite words to rhyme was "gherkin," as in "pickle." Dad thought of a loitering pickle—a "lurkin' gherkin"—a saucy pickle—a "smirkin' gherkin"—a busy pickle—a "workin' gherkin."

Sign Alphabet Race was my mother's game contribution. You had to go through the alphabet, finding each letter from a word on a road sign that began with that letter, so for *A* you might see a sign that read "Alfalfa Farm Ahead," and there was your *A*. License plates didn't count. *Q*'s and *X*'s and *Z*'s created a frenzy, and we learned to look for "Quality," "X-tra," and "Zoo" whenever possible. The first person to finish the alphabet was the winner.

Dad mostly drove, Mom sat shotgun, and Geoff and I took the backseat, no seat belts, and I sometimes slouched down and shoved my knees up against the back of the driver's seat and drifted off into daydreams about the Beatles, and further down into motion induced sleep, waking up that much nearer to our destination. My parents called it "racking off the miles."

When we weren't playing games or sleeping on these car trips, we were singing. We had a perfect little quartet. You've perhaps heard the song "Daddy Sang Bass (Mama sang tenor, / Me and little brother would join right in there . . .)," and really, that was us. For some reason, no matter what time of year it was (and it was nearly always summer, which was vacation time), we sang Christmas carols. All of us having sung in the church choir, I suppose this was the material we were not only the most familiar with but had the most sophistication at as a group. The Gloria refrain of "Angels We Have Heard on High," for example, included not only harmony but counterpoint melody, which I proudly provided. Mother sang lead, Geoff alto, Daddy did sing bass, and I sang a third above Mother.

Even though both my parents were big music lovers and had

talent, neither of them pursued it professionally. We came from a place where that just wasn't done. We were not Hollywood or New York; we were practical midwesterners. But I take pride in the fact that both my parents challenged themselves academically after we children were born, Mother especially. At forty-four she got a master's degree in education. And then she went to law school a year later. With her law degree, she worked as the assistant state's attorney in the D.A.'s office before starting her own successful family-law practice. Mom was a great defense attorney and an even finer prosecutor, and for this my father nicknamed her "Killer Barb."

Mother graduating from law school, 1973

My mother made our clothes because her mother made her clothes, and she loved sewing, actually, and the economy in it. She made us matching mother-daughter dresses. One that I remember was a coral cotton print with a repeating Parisian cityscape and a tight bodice with a full circle skirt, fifties style. Another was made of navy and white dotted swiss. My mother made beautiful clothes, and it's her fault that I have a clothes fetish. When I finally needed a training bra, we were forced to shop. I couldn't believe my eyes. There was rack after rack of ready-made clothes—and I couldn't have any of them. That night I dreamed I got up one morning and all the exquisite things I had seen at the store were draped over my bed, on chairs, from hangers, a cornucopia of new-with-tags, honest-to-goodness store-bought clothes. This is probably the earliest sign of the retail maniac I would someday become.

Mother grew up in Mount Vernon, South Dakota, born to Esther and Homer Croson. She was one of eight children in a three-room house in a one-horse town. Her father was a mailman. Her mother raised the children and baked the bread and sewed the clothing, and these things anchored my mother, because at twenty years old she gave up college and her dreams of singing and writing poetry to marry my father and have children. Like her mother, she baked bread and sewed our clothes and cleaned house and took us to church on Sundays.

My parents were barely out of high school when they met and married, and they had my brother inside a year, then me. My mom was twenty-three when she had me; my dad was twenty-five. She had us, she raised us, she made our home, and she stood by Dad as he uprooted the family twice in order to get his Ph.D. My mother cared, she cared terribly, perhaps she cared too much. She was caught between having the gift of compassion and the curse of concern for appearances. And Mother believed she could or should control it all, fix it, make it right, make it perfect.

As a kid I so loved my mother. I wanted my mother to think I was the greatest girl on earth. She was perfect. She was gracious and kind and kept herself up. She was soothing and calm. Mother even drank her coffee with her little pinkie out. I thought she must know everything. I thought she was magic. With Mother everything would be all right. She had supernatural powers.

Mother had grace. She's small-boned and delicate. She never moved with urgency or lost her temper except to say "Fudge!" now and then if she accidentally burned or cut herself or chipped a nail. Her hands were of great pride to her, and to this day she continually puts on hand lotion and files her nails, which are always polished to perfection. Her smile was warm and bright white and dazzling, and as a girl she was downright stunning in a Katharine Hepburn sort of way, with shiny curled hair and cheekbones for days. When she stood, she did so like a ballet dancer, posture perfect. Mother dressed crisply in the clothes she made for herself, whether she was going out for cocktails or gardening. To this day she may indulge in a sip of wine or beer. I remember when you could buy Miller in mini seven-ounce bottles—my mother would drink half of one, cap it, and place it back in the fridge.

I loved my mother, and I knew I would never be as wonderful as she was. I was awkward and careless, always fretting and worried over something. I had snarly hair and a space between my teeth. I played in the mud and dug up the flower garden to make hollyhock dolls. My white anklet socks for church fell down and got caught in the heels of my patent-leather shoes. I was scared of thunder. I was scared of dying. I was scared of the dark. And I was willful.

My mother had a different daughter in mind, I think, certainly a child more malleable and refined. Someone more like my older brother, Geoff, a model kid, smart as a whip and eager to please. He seemed to possess a certain sophistication right from the get-go. Geoff studied classical violin in favor of the guitar. While I grudgingly took piano lessons, it was the Beatles, not Bach, who snared me.

Now, my dad, he's a performer. Dad has always held court with jokes and one-liners and philosophical tidbits. He's got advanced Alzheimer's now and can't remember my name, but at lunch in the Memory Unit the other day I sat with him as the Hispanic attendant cleared his plate. "Are you feenish?" she asked, and my dad, not missing a beat, replied, "No, I'm German." Which he's not, but that's not the point. Dad has a quick wit. My mother especially likes a comment I made in frustration once to Dad as he was milking me for attention. "React! React!" I shouted. And it stuck.

Although he got his doctorate in psychology, he chose not to practice but to teach—another form of performance. My father had a guitar and a banjo and longed to be a member of the Kingston Trio the way I would long to be a Beatle. He and a couple of his friends would convene in the backyard from time to time, donning matching short-sleeved striped, button-down shirts and play their favorites by the trio. Dad taught me a few basic chords on the guitar, and I fell in love with it. Yes, I got blisters and my fingers bled, but no matter. Although I had been taking piano lessons since I was six, I soon lost interest. The guitar seemed made for me, and the ring of each painfully learned chord was a thrill. I was ten, it was 1966. It was Dad who gave me this.

And it was Dad who had a hair-trigger temper. To this day he can furrow his brow in a way that still makes me shudder, although now it is nothing but mock anger, another joke. He even growls at the ladies in the Memory Unit to make them laugh. But I knew him when it wasn't funny. I don't know where it came from.

Dad as General MacArthur, 1966

Was my grandfather an angry person? Dad got it from some-where. "It" was chasing me around the house in order to pin me down and smell my breath to determine if I had in fact stolen my brother's peppermint candy. "It" was wrenching me from the chair at the kitchen table when I sassed, my feet catching under-neath and dragging the chair across the linoleum, or pushing me against walls if I left the basement door open. It was Dad who sang me to sleep on the couch in the living room in front of the fire. And Dad who grew so frustrated with me for waking my mother up in the night that he kept me awake all night once, so I could "see what it felt like." I was six years old.

I can't help but think that my dad saw himself in me to a

certain extent, which seemed both bad and good. Dad and I competed for attention; we were both headstrong smart-asses, passionate and volatile. Now, being a parent myself, I know that when you see your kids mirror back your personality and behavior, it's interesting but not always positive. If anyone in the Colvin family is prone to having outbursts like my father, it's me. I don't exactly see stars, but I can become pretty angry. Mostly in my relationships with men, which I'll get into later.

When I think of my dad, I see his shit-eating grin. I see his compact, taut body bent over a banjo or a sailboat or a power saw. I see the delight on his face at my imitation of LBJ. I see the black thunderhead of his temper blow in after we once again break the sprinkler by running through it in the hot midwestern summer.

Dad and me, 1986

Dad loved a project in the garage, whether it was restoring a sports car or designing a canoe or building anything from the family-room couch to model airplanes to the bomb shelter on Canby Street. His uniform was jeans, a T-shirt, and a yellow canvas Windbreaker that was covered in all manner of wood stains and glue globs and dirt and oil. My mother tried to throw it away about fifteen years ago, but I rescued it. Somehow that Windbreaker is my father to me. When I think of my dad, he is a full garment, the color of the sun, marred by rips and stains and sweat. He seems always in pursuit of something and never quite getting it. He was by turns charming and fun-loving and ferocious, at once lovable and fearsome, and I never knew which trait to put my faith in.

When I was six, my sister, Kay, dethroned me. I have a photograph of me in my new homemade polyester Chinese pajamas curled around her little bouncing baby chair. She's gazing up in wide-eyed wonderment, and I look totally forlorn. My sister has gorgeous wavy black hair, and my mother would put it up in a ponytail, twist Kay's damp hair around her finger and slink the finger out, magically leaving a perfect ringlet. My hair was mousy brown and straight and always so full of tangles that my mother finally lost it one day, took me to the beauty shop, and had it all cut off with the shortest bangs imaginable. If memory serves, I resembled Richard Harris in *Camelot*, minus the goatee. The sibling rivalry was rather Laura Ingalls Wilder–esque, which is fitting given our Dakota birthplace, and hair really is so all-important. Kay got the goods there. She was also blessed with a willowy build, and she tanned easily, and for all of this I found many ways to torture her, like showing her a little scab that came off my knee and telling her it was a burned potato chip so she would eat it.

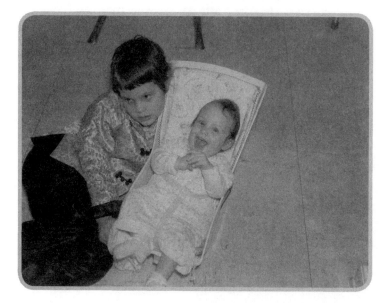

New sister, new pajamas, 1961

I am six years older, but I wasn't much of a big sister to Kay. I didn't know her very well until much later in our lives. It's as though Geoff and I came as a matched pair and Kay and Clay came as another. My little brother, Clay, might be the most well adjusted out of all of us, save for the fact that he designs fighter jets for Lockheed Martin. But he also raises bonsai trees and is one of the dying breed of true gentlemen. Anyway, Kay and Clay had their world, Geoff and I had ours, and the two did not intersect. I'd moved out of the house by the time my sister was eleven and my little brother was eight. I was not really a witness to their growing up, nor did I even care to be.

Christmas card, 1972, in the canoe and pool Dad built

I moved to New York in 1980 when I was twenty-four and Kay was eighteen. My family drove up to give me some furniture, and Kay came along. She had finally grown into someone I could relate to. Her first morning there, we walked to the Greek coffee shop on the corner to get coffee. The cashier, upon seeing us, smiled and said, "There is no doubt what you are to each other."

Apparently we had become a matched pair, and in the ensuing years we've sometimes been hard to tell apart.

She began to write me letters from Austin, where she was attending college, and I would call or write back. I had a new friend. This meant the world to me, because I felt there was the possibility that someone in my family might regard me as more than troubled and neurotic. Kay liked me. She needed my friendship, too. We each needed a sister.

Our pet names for each other are "Fine" and "Violet." The first was born from our salutations to each other when we wrote letters: "Dear fine yon sister" or "Dearest fine one." This evolved simply into "Fine." (Hello, Fine, how are you?) We developed our own language based on movie quotes, and this brought us to "Violet." *It's a Wonderful Life* is required viewing for us at Christmastime, and much of our dialogue is taken from it ("My mouth's bleedin', Burt! My mouth's bleedin'!")—most notably from an early scene at the drugstore where the young George Bailey, a soda jerk, greets the prettiest girl in school as she comes in to flirt with him: "H'lo, Violet." Soon every phone call began this way. "H'lo, Violet." Now we are Violet. And Vi. And Yer Vi. We've both lived in Austin now for fifteen years, and our daughters, the cousins, have grown up together. And although I may be the songwriter, it's my sister, Kay, who developed our language and our nicknames, and she might say at this point, "Violet, there'll be nary a dry eye!"

I got my mother's cheekbones and mouth, my dad's nose and eyes. My build resembles my father's, solid and sinewy. My singing is a neat combination of the two of them—I inherited the dexterity of my mother's trained, operatic-type voice and the earthy, just-us-folks warmth of my father's delivery. I walk like a cowboy. I'm bound by deep love to my family and would do anything they asked of me. As my siblings and I got older, the gaps seemed to close, but growing up I sometimes felt like we were satellites, orbiting the planet of our parents, sending and receiving necessary information at regular intervals but ultimately alone out in space. To an extent, though, this has always been my nature—feeling apart from. Things would get worse for me before they got better.

2
A Vengeance

Me at ten, with a space between my teeth and a bad hair day, 1966

**You don't have to drag me down,
I descend.**

The trouble mostly started when I was twelve, after the family moved from Vermillion to London, Ontario, briefly, and then on to Carbondale, Illinois. I was a simple geek in South Dakota, a cool cat in Canada, and a total freak show in Illinois—that was the general progression.

From as far back as I can remember, I have been afflicted with phobias of a hypochondriac's nature. From the flu to flesh-eating viruses to good old predictable brain cancer, I've spent more than my fair share of time worrying about what I might die of. I drove my poor mother crazy by asking her constantly, "Will I be all right?" This has been diagnosed as "panic disorder," but for me it's just been a general way of life. I was neurotic, anxious, headstrong, emotional, overly sensitive, and high-maintenance. (Haven't changed much . . .) I took a lot of energy. I was afraid of dying. I was afraid of getting sick. I was simply afraid. I don't know if it was the mood disorder already in play or if I was just that kind of kid. Maybe it was a combination of both.

In 1967, when I was eleven, my father sold the small newspaper business he had inherited from his father and decided to go back to college to get a doctorate in psychology, so wherever his schooling took him, we followed. I'd lived in Vermillion my whole life, and I was terrified at the prospect of leaving. But leave we did. First stop: Canada!

We moved into a split-level ranch house in the suburbs of London, Ontario, on Hunt Village Crescent, just down the street from a popular girl named Tara who befriended me. As fate would have it, my status as "new girl" worked in my favor; plus, I had breasts by that time and was becoming almost pretty after my awkward, space-between-my-teeth-with-hairy-legs phase. I had my first-ever male teacher, Mr. Waite, who had red hair and a killer smile. I was in love with him, so of course I made an ass of myself all the time, most poignantly when he read the morning prayer over my shoulder one day and I realized after he walked away that on the back of my hand (which was palm down, holding the book open) was a monstrous booger.

Me, Dad, and Geoff, 1967

Canada worked out for me. It was very clean and had candy bars far superior to those in the States. One of my favorite memories is of skiing on winter weekends and enjoying the après-ski treat of a Cadbury's Crunchie bar and a hot chocolate. A boy named Robbie liked me, and my mother actually *bought* me an outfit from Eaton's Department Store—a navy blue wool skirt and a green, orange, and navy striped sweater vest. I reveled in my good fortune for a scant year, but Dad burned my little playhouse down when he announced we were moving again, to Carbondale, Illinois, where by the middle of seventh grade, at the age of twelve, I would become a bag lady.

Carbondale is a funky town in southern Illinois whose claim to fame is its large university, where my father opted to finish his degree. Carbondale held no charm for me; I'll just come right out and say it. None of us liked it very much. We made fun of it. The way people talked and their accents and even the name were so . . . unpoetic.

The town bordered Kentucky, Missouri, and Tennessee and had the humidity and summer heat to prove it, which I vividly recall because we arrived in July. We took up residence on a cul-de-sac called Norwood Drive, situated on the outskirts of some woods that separated us from the upscale part of town. I'd never been around strip malls, Walmart, or Arby's before. Vermillion was too small, Canada too smart. And I'd never experienced a southern accent either, which to me just sounded stupid. Now, having lived in Texas awhile, I've changed my mind, but Texas and southern Illinois are a bit different culturally, trust me. Of course, I made friendships there that would last a lifetime, a lesson worth noting. During some of the unhappiest times of my life, I've made some of my best friends.

None of this was obvious to me that blazing-hot summer, and I dreaded my first day of school. I had discovered a Top 40 radio station called KXOK out of St. Louis and was deeply immersed in the hits of that summer, such as "Everyday People," "Gentle on My Mind," "Get Back," "Honky Tonk Women," and "Just Dropped In (to See What Condition My Condition Was In)." But the unlikely song, if you can call it that, that stands out in my memory, the song that brought me to tears every time, was a jingle for Thom McAn shoes:

> *Yesterday they took away my window,*
> *But I can still see things my way.*
> *Don't let them tell you what you can do.*
> *Do your own thing, do your own thing today.*

To this day it's one of the only jingles I've ever heard that was not only plaintive but in a minor key, surely a misguided notion by someone at Thom McAn, but it worked for me, especially the sentiment that "yesterday they took away my window." Which was Canada.

I do remember finding something good even in the isolation I felt after we moved to Carbondale that July. I knew absolutely no one, and the prospect of school terrified me, but in those two remaining months of summer, before I was to start school, I discovered how much I loved to be alone in the house. It was the time I could really sing, whether it was along with Lulu on "To Sir with Love," or the words I made up to the classical pieces I knew on piano. "Minuet in G," for example, went like this:

> *When the Minuet in G is played,*
> *People dance and parade.*
> *When the Minuet in G is played,*
> *Watch the people dance and then parade.*
> *What I've heard of this song*
> *It is very good,*
> *Good for listening.*
> *When the Minuet in G is played,*
> *People dance and parade.*

So I guess even way back then, at least part of me wanted to write songs, even though I hadn't yet heard my songwriting heroes, the ones who would define the genre I would come to want to inhabit.

I could easily entertain myself for hours while alone at home, just singing and playing and blasting the stereo or the radio. It was always terrific news when the rest of the family would head off to Walmart and I was allowed to have my own, private world of music.

But soon the wretched day came when it was time for me to start school. What had happened to me? I'd managed the transition reasonably well in Canada, but I felt as if only a limited amount of luck had been allotted to me thus far and that with the move to Carbondale it had run out. I had no faith, none, in myself, in my family, in whomever I might meet, in the teachers I would have. The really odd thing is that I was right.

I was to take a bus, another first, to Lincoln Junior High School, a massive brick structure just east of downtown Carbondale that housed the town's entire seventh and eighth grades. There I had the misfortune of being assigned to the meanest teacher who ever drew breath. He was given to throwing erasers and chalk, barking lessons to us in his pinched voice like the army sergeant he once was, crew cut and all, and reading his paycheck aloud to us every Friday. Mercenary? Pshaw.

There was also corporal punishment at Lincoln, and we had one specific hall monitor, a gigantic hulk of a man who would slowly stroll down the halls, chuckling as he whacked a ruler against his palm. I swear the place felt like a lockdown facility. I was twelve years old, a time when bodies and minds and hearts go through so much, and I was simply not equipped for this passage. The passage had to do with the big, bad world, and I wasn't ready to be in it—the mean teachers; the ominous, punitive hall monitor; the jaded, cruel kids; the sheer size and breadth of the humanity. I'd attended two small schools in my life, and I had thin skin.

My mother was standing in the garage when I came home that first day. I'd held it in until then, but when I saw her, my mouth opened and no sound came out. I was sobbing so hard I simply put my head on her shoulder and drooled down her back. She was devastated to see me in such misery, yet surely it was something I would get used to and get over. But it wasn't. I was literally Lincoln Junior High School–phobic. It felt like a cold, vast, prison, and I was a new inmate. I just couldn't figure out what my crime was. The panic attacks started every morning in homeroom. All I wanted was to go home, back to my music world, back to my mother. I couldn't take it. I began to feel dizzy and anxious, and I started calling Mom within the first weeks of school to come and get me because I felt sick. We had, I think, a white station wagon, and my little brother, Clay, must have been in the car, since he couldn't have been more than three then and Mom stayed home with him. How often did I ask her to come get me? Once a week? It seemed like every day. For a while she would do it, and I don't remember her being mad about it. When I was home, I became addicted to soap operas like *Love Is a Many Splendored Thing*. I read books and played the guitar. I was learning Simon & Garfunkel, specifically "April Come She Will" and "Flowers Never Bend with the Rainfall" and "The Dangling Conversation."

I was taken to the doctor to figure out what was wrong, but they couldn't find anything. So eventually my mom felt she had no choice but to refuse to pick me up anymore. It was my job to go to school—something I tell my own daughter—and it was their job to make me go. But once it became a battle, we were all screwed. Maybe I could have been homeschooled for a time. Or maybe a deal could have been struck whereby I would go to Lincoln for part of the day but not all. But there was simply no insight into my heart except to regard me as rebellious. Later my mother told me, "We didn't know what to do. We couldn't take anything away from you except television, because you had no friends and never went anywhere," the implication being that punitive measures were the natural course of action, and at that time I suppose they were. I was in over my head, and so were my parents.

I got creative, holding a thermometer against a lightbulb to feign fever. That wore itself out, too, and I knew that if I were to keep avoiding school, I'd have to up the ante. I would ask a teacher if I could use the bathroom, excuse myself, and just leave the building. I didn't play hooky to do something fun. I would have preferred to be home with my mother. I'd wander the streets of Carbondale for a few hours and at around three-thirty I'd go home, where no one was the wiser until the school started calling there when I'd go missing. Sometimes I would leave school between periods and not go home at all until after dark, when I would lurk around the house until one of my parents came out and found me. After that I was driven to school every morning, where the staff was instructed to keep an eye on me at all times. I still found ways to get out.

One of my favorite places to go was the strip mall near our house. There was a Santa Claus shack stored in the back alley, behind the supermarket. The Santa shack was a little building where Santa would take up residence in front of the grocery store at Christmastime, but it was kept out in back the rest of the year. I would go to the store, buy a bag of caramels and a crossword-puzzle book, head for the alley, and hang out in the Santa shack, having put on several layers of clothes, given that it was winter, and resembling nothing so much as a twelve-year-old homeless girl. I might just as well have had a grocery cart loaded with empty cans. But I did have a home.

I suppose the worry to my parents was at a breaking point. In fact, I recently learned that a photo of me from that year, a black-and-white portrait that was taken by a professional, was arranged for the express purpose of identifying me should I really run away, or worse.

Me at twelve—photo taken in case I ran away—1968

The pinnacle of this situation occurred that winter, after I'd played out every trick, both at home and at school. Either Mother or Dad was driving me to school in the mornings now to ensure a safe delivery. So one day I got up before anyone else in the house, while it was still dark, and left. Around the side of the house was the pop-up camper trailer we used to take on vacations. It was all folded up for the winter, but there was still a small door you could open to crawl into. I let myself into the cramped space between the two benches and in front of the cupboards inside the trailer. I locked the door from within, and I stayed there. It was cold and dark and tiny, and it was better than going to school. Anything was better than going to school. I heard footsteps in the crunchy snow as my dad came out to look for me. He even tried the door on the camper, but I had locked it, and he didn't pursue that idea.

I stayed and stayed. I stayed so long that I peed on myself. I was afraid to get out, because I knew I'd have been made to go to school. A war had begun, and neither my parents nor I had figured on my being so formidable an opponent. Finally I estimated that enough time had elapsed and that school must be over. I crawled out of the camper, my legs hardly able to stand, and saw that the sun was heading west. So it was afternoon, and I'd dodged another day at school. I began my walk to the Santa shack, but a neighbor saw me, put me in her car, and brought me back home. My mother was there, and so was my father. When he saw me, he got that look, the dark scowl that meant he was extremely displeased and that most probably sparks would fly. And sure enough, Dad grabbed me by the arm and began to drag me to the car. It was only two-thirty. There was still an hour of school left, and he wanted to make sure I got there. But my mother stopped him. Did she smell the urine on my clothes? She stopped him and gave me something to eat.

My hiding place, 1966

It's ironic that my father was studying psychology during this time and didn't see what was happening to me, but you have to understand he was a Skinner man. It was all about behavior and positive and negative reinforcement, usually with M&M's as I recall. Clearly what I was doing did not fall neatly under the heading of behavior that should be positively reinforced. No M&M's for me. My father decided the only way to deal with me was to reverse the lock on my bedroom door and nail my windows shut when I went to bed at night. He would let me out in the morning and drive me to school, where he and my mother would take turns waiting outside each of my classrooms and walking me to the next one.

Given their strict midwestern upbringing, and what had to have been the limitations of their youth, my parents didn't have a lot of resources available to them regarding a child like me. Nowadays we've got kid shrinks galore and private schools and Ritalin, but back then it came down to a battle of wills. Not giving up without a fight became my fallback position, even after I was long gone from my parents' jurisdiction.

My parents did send me to a therapist, but of him I recall very little. What seemed to help the most was my father's telling me that if I would sew my own clothes, he would buy me all the fabric I wanted. I'd never had all of anything I ever wanted before, and I loved clothes—I still love clothes. And thanks to Mom, I could sew. I'd watch the clock at school as the day wore on, counting the minutes until three-thirty, when Mom would take me to the fabric store and I could indulge myself. I got into a matching-bolero-and-skirt phase, and I bought tweedy wools and lawn stripes and would work up in my mother's sewing room after school as the winter days grew darker, until I was called down to dinner.

I fell in with some girls at school—Gwen Geyer, Gail Parrish, and Peggy Cochran. They thought I was strange but befriended me anyway. I was the kid who didn't want to go to school, whose parents had to accompany her to class. But between therapy and the sewing and the girls, I began to be able to tolerate Lincoln Junior High. I was allowed to stop going to therapy. It was enough that I was sent. There would be plenty more to come anyway.

In the spring, with all the determination I could muster, I managed a perfect attendance record, wearing the bright paisley peasant dresses I'd made during that season in hell. The homeless girl was home again, at least for a while.

3
She Opened a Book

Geoff playing the guitar I learned on, 1963

I live on a dream, it came to me when I was young.

When I was fourteen, I designed my first album cover. It was a pencil drawing of two eyes, one open and one closed, with a tear falling from the closed eye. I thought it was very deep.

The guitar had permanent residence at the foot of my bed, and when trouble came in the form of panic or pain, I reached for the guitar. I really turned a corner when I started to play. I didn't have to be in the church choir or sing along to a record with a hairbrush microphone anymore. I could produce something totally complete with my voice and the guitar. I found my instrument and, along with it, another part of myself. I was becoming a musician.

I learned "This Land Is Your Land" and understood by ear the general relationship of a key and the basic one, four, and five chords that went with it. With the help of a Mel Bay guitar book, I taught myself chords by attempting to play "This Land Is Your Land" in every key. I learned to play on a Harmony guitar with four strings, and then my parents got me a six-string Yamaha one Christmas. The first song I recall figuring out on my own—and this is infinitely embarrassing—was a Great Shakes commercial:

> *Any place can be your soda fountain now,*
> *With Great Shakes, new Great Shakes.*
> *Mix it up with milk and make a real thick shake,*
> *With Great Shakes, new Great Shakes . . .*

It had sort of a Beach Boys–meets–Peter, Paul and Mary feel to it, and I confess to being somewhat smitten. Thankfully, I soon progressed to tackling some Beatles, Bob Dylan, and Judy Collins. I suppose I could have learned these songs on piano, but the guitar was better. "Blowin' in the Wind" on piano was so cheesy. The same goes for "I've Just Seen a Face." When I got home from school, I'd eat some ice cream or saltine crackers and peanut butter, talk on the phone, write poetry. Then I'd play the guitar, in my bedroom or sometimes in the living room. I didn't hide my playing and singing; they were part of the sound track of the house.

I met some other kids who played guitar, too. We learned old folk songs like "All My Trials" off my father's Kingston Trio records, complete with counterpoint melody. "Sounds of Silence" was huge for us. In fact, Simon & Garfunkel were a real mainstay, but our big hit was "Atlantis" by Donovan. We couldn't wait for the end and the anthemic refrain of "Way down below the ocean, where I wanna be, she may be . . ." The beginning of the song was all talking, and it was kind of a chore to get through. And no one wanted to chirp "Hail, Atlantis!" but the ending was worth it.

My friend Janey's older sister, Robin, introduced me to Laura Nyro. Then, at summer church camp, an older girl (fifteen) told me point-blank to get "Clouds" by Joni Mitchell. It was like an edict, should I ever want to understand *anything*. Not since the Beatles had my world been so shaken by music. Joanne, my closest guitar-playing pal, and I set out to learn Joni Mitchell's entire catalog, but because Joni never played in standard tuning, we were stymied. Then a miracle occurred. Joanne met a college student named Vicki who gave guitar lessons at the local music shop—*and she knew Joni Mitchell tunings.* We practically moved in with her. The code was cracked, and the gates of heaven flew open.

Joanne and I took turns meeting at each other's house, all through junior high and high school. We played "Rocky Mountain High," "I Ain't Marchin' Anymore" by Phil Ochs, Joni Mitchell's "Conversation" and "Chelsea Morning," "Someday Soon" and "My Father" by Judy Collins, and Leonard Cohen's "Suzanne," as sung by Judy Collins. Joanne had an older sister, Tina, and she could sing, so sometimes we'd add a third part.

There are artists who just seem to spring out of the wild with a ready-made vibe, but most of us have to copy people for a long time in hopes of developing our own style. James Taylor was one of those artists who seemed to have emerged fully formed. I remember baby-sitting one night when Janey tore over with the 45 of "Fire and Rain," insisting that the second coming had arrived—and she was right.

Me and Liz, 1975

Me and Joanne, 1975

Jane, 1975

I went through this phase of writing songs when I was fourteen or so. I'd fallen in love with a guy who didn't know I was alive, so I channeled my unrequited love into songs. I ended up writing maybe ten. They were based primarily on Joni Mitchell and Laura Nyro songs. Some were about being home, at my parents', and feeling misunderstood. I can still remember some of the titles: "Hey, J," "Tell the Clouds to All Come Home," "I Want War," and "Thought of You." They're not anything I would play now, but back then I played them for Joanne, Liz, Mandy, and Jane. Joanne was writing songs, too.

My repertoire was expanding, and I actually got a gig at a hippie-dippy student church called the Newman Center in Carbondale when I was fifteen. I think I played Joni Mitchell, "He's a Runner" by Laura Nyro, James Taylor, and Simon & Garfunkel.

After my set I was too jazzed to quit, and my meager audience followed me into the ladies' bathroom, where the acoustics rocked. But, mostly, more and more of us got together just to play, in our rooms, at Saturday-night church youth group get-togethers, and whenever our parents had parties.

I took my guitar to school often, and I'd play with my friends, sometimes outside on the lawn at lunchtime or in one of the listening-room cubicles in study hall. Joanne and I even managed to sneak our guitars into French class, further goading poor Miss Crow, the most tortured teacher in the whole school. Phil Ochs, Dylan, John Denver, Cat Stevens, Dan Fogelberg, Elton John. Crosby, Stills, Nash & Young. Jackson Browne. I learned songs by Linda Ronstadt, Bonnie Raitt, and the Eagles and realized that this guy Jackson was doing the same material. I thought, *Wow, this fellow has good taste.* When I finally put it together that he had *written* this stuff, I fell totally in love with him.

There was no shortage of songs any of us wanted to learn. They were endless. We'd show one another different things. We'd work them out on our own and show one another what we'd learned. I knew that I was fast; I was a quick study. I had a good ear; I could hear when things were in tune and out of tune. And I knew I had a good voice, maybe one of the better ones. As a sophomore I auditioned for the school musical by playing the guitar and singing a song from *Camelot:* "I Loved You Once in Silence." The Vanessa Redgrave–Richard Harris film was popular at the time, and we were all pretty into it. I knew the musicals really well from my parents' albums. And I got the lead: Eliza in *My Fair Lady.* The next year I got the lead again: Anna in *The King and I.* Musicals required a lot of rehearsal, late into the evening, and my parents were supportive about it. They were very proud. To this day I have performance-anxiety dreams about acting.

I was like a train. My recollection is that this is just what I was meant to do. I didn't feel I had to ask permission. My parents bought me a reel-to-reel tape recorder for Christmas when I was around fourteen or fifteen. It was a big present. I didn't ask for it— they somehow knew I wanted it. The way they gave it to me was that they hid it under a table in the living room and it was running all Christmas morning, and the end of that tape is me finding the tape recorder and screaming. I knew, of course, that it was for me.

I was the only one of my friends who had one. And I could overdub on it. It was kind of intricate; it was difficult to do, but you could do it. I taught myself so I could overdub myself singing harmony. I still have some of those tapes. I had my friends sing with me on it, too. We sang the Beatles' "If I Fell" in three-part harmony.

It's not easy to adequately describe my feelings about this period of time and my musical development. Playing and learning and listening were my whole life. When I went to sleep at night, I always played the same Laura Nyro song—"Save the Country." It was my lullaby. When I heard "Friends" by Elton John and saw the film of the same name, it spoke to all my notions about rebellious youth and feeling misunderstood and the deep, deep connection I had with my friends, who really became my family all through high school. The song made me weep from the deepest place inside me. I played it again and again, a sort of cleansing therapy, a sense of belonging, and all the music I loved did that.

I pored over every album cover, memorizing the lyrics, the players, even the photographers. The whole scene was a fairy tale. I was transfixed, obsessed, and, looking back, I realize I was also lucky. How much more fortunate could I have been, that the first album I ever got was *Meet the Beatles*? That in fourth grade I bought *Rubber Soul*? How lucky was I to grow up in the singer-songwriter heyday? Using the money I saved from baby-sitting, I eventually bought my dream guitar, a Martin D-28, the gold standard. I felt how some guys must feel about a car.

My first concert was Judy Collins in Edwardsville, Illinois.

I was probably thirteen or fourteen. My parents took me and Joanne, and I remember my father, as we sat on the lawn pretending to get high from the secondhand pot smoke. Judy was a hero of mine—"Someday Soon" was a staple in my arsenal, thanks to my folks, and I learned lots of songs off her records.

Next I saw Simon & Garfunkel at the arena at Southern Illinois University. I believe I was fifteen and enough of a fan that I recognized Paul's brother, Eddie, who walked into the audience before the show started. Like an idiot punk, I yelled, "Hey, Eddie!" I got him to look and then hid. I had made contact! If only with a blood relative.

The first time I saw James Taylor was at the SIU arena as well. He played solo. I had pretty good seats and the undeniable feeling that he would sense my presence and ask me to sing with him. It must have slipped his mind. If you had told me then that I would someday *meet* James Taylor, much less sing with him or kiss his cheek, for God's sake, I would have absolutely died right on the spot, but then I wouldn't have lived to meet Joni Mitchell and gotten to tell her about the necklace I made for her in 1974 and how I gave it to a roadie after her show in St. Louis with a note and express orders to deliver it to her. It was kind of endearingly naïve of me. I wouldn't have gotten to ask her the question that had burned in me for years: Did anyone else notice, or was I the only one, that on the cover of *Hejira* her left arm looks like an erect penis? I had no sooner begun to mention it to her when she piped right up and said, "Oh, the cock!" So my mind could finally rest.

I also wouldn't have gotten to sing with Jackson Browne or David Crosby and Graham Nash and Neil Young or Judy Collins or Bonnie Raitt. I wouldn't have met Paul Simon or Elton John or Laura Nyro—or Paul McCartney.

But I'm getting ahead of myself. There were a lot of miles to go before those dreams, like many others, stood a chance of coming true.

4
Get the Kids

High school, 1971

Hey everybody in the old schoolyard,
We took it all the way and we took it hard.

By the time I started high school in Carbondale, I had trans-
formed my image from chronic truant to hip folkie girl with
guitar. Music was my identity, and it served me well. From there

I could branch out. And thanks to my earlier stint as a bag lady, my skills at sneaking out of the house were well honed. Plus, I had discovered boys, oh, yes, yes, yes.

I know there has been speculation that I might be gay, but listen, it's just not true. I liked boys, period, and still do, although sometimes I've wanted to be gay, believe me. The summer of my fourteenth year, I had my first big crush on an older man, fifteen, who played guitar and thought himself to be all that and a bag of chips. I thought so, too. He came to my open window in the middle of the night (they weren't nailed shut anymore) and beckoned me come hither. I promptly crawled out the window and walked to his house with him, where I lost my virginity in the basement. Good, now *that* was done. Onward.

The next boy I liked was a dreamboat named Mick, a true bohemian and absolutely adorable. For some reason I wouldn't go "all the way" with him. I guess I wanted to learn the finer points of sex, like foreplay. I had to ride my bike to and from his house, where I would crawl up some latticework to his bedroom window. Some of my fondest memories are those rides, before and after the clandestine thrills with Mick, in the still dark when everyone else was asleep and the streets were mine, with not a single sound except the whir of my bicycle tires.

Rollie was my first real boyfriend, my best boyfriend. I don't know what it says about me that I chose best when I was fifteen. I guess things were inherently easier in a way, with all of us still living at home and being pretty carefree for the most part. Rollie was good stuff, a good man. He came to our high school my freshman year from Minnesota and was an army brat who hailed from too many places to count, including Australia, which gave him great mystery. He told me he cared for me the day school was out my freshman year, the same year Janis Joplin and Jimi Hendrix died, the year the Beatles and Simon & Garfunkel broke up, the year the movie *Woodstock* came out. My life changed overnight. I had a true companion. We became inseparable. We were friends and lovers. We took care of each other.

There was one particular night that Rollie had dropped me off at home when after I got into the house I went to the front-room window to watch him drive away. He must have seen me, because he backed up, sat for a moment, and pulled away again. I didn't move. He backed up again, sat in the car, drove away. And again. Over and over. I don't know how many times that night he did this dance with me, but I'll never forget it.

My parents found out that Rollie and I were having sex. I guess we started that about six months into the relationship. It was a big step for us and well planned for. I got birth-control pills from the free clinic. My mother discovered them. The shit hit the fan. Rollie was summoned over, and my father had a private talk with him in his office. One of our friends came to pick him up at some point, and he was ushered out the door in tears. I'm not sure why my parents were so upset. I wasn't going to get pregnant. And they loved Rollie.

But that's actually very shortsighted of me. In retrospect, this certainly defines not only the core of my own disconnect with my parents but perhaps the alienation of my whole generation. I was just a little bit shy of the Age of Aquarius, but its principles seemed sound to me—all you need is love. Rollie and I had love, we were hurting no one, we were responsible. But, of course, this came smack up against the morals of my parents' generation, which dictated that premarital sex was wrong. Isn't it always the case? These days I'm stunned when my daughter tells me, "It's chill, Mom," after I hear Snoop Dogg rapping about squeezing Katy Perry's buns. I grew up in the era of *the* generation gap. Naturally my parents were the enemy.

In addition, there was something personally askew between my parents and me. Today I can look back and understand the challenges I presented to these two very young people who were fantastically underprepared to raise a rebel, an artist, a depressive. Today I can see that so much of life is timing, that my folks and I are more alike than any of us could have imagined. Both of them are artists who chose other paths. My father also rebelled as a young man, and my mother waited until she was a grown woman and knew her enemies, which were and are the systems that threatened her rights and those of her children, of all children. It's true that perhaps my mother has never taken a mental-health day in her life, but Dad takes Prozac and has phobias like me and my sister. Back then, though, all they could detect was nonconformity and trouble, and all I could sense was that my very self was somehow just wrong.

So they told Rollie and me that we couldn't see each other anymore. There was not a worse thing they could have chosen to do to me. Rollie was such a balancing force in my life. He got along with Mom and Dad, so I could, too. He was a Christian Scientist, and I was a hypochondriac. He used to tell me, "Shawny, there is no spot where God is not, for God is everywhere." And my stomachache would subside, my heart would stop racing.

I woke up the next morning, after we'd been separated, and a storm was blowing in. I'd also been grounded in order to minimize the chance of our seeing each other on the sly. My windows might just have been nailed shut again. I went out to our backyard and sat on top of the picnic table. I sat and watched the storm blow in, and I can't explain it, but somehow I knew, deep down, that it would be all right.

I felt stripped and shaken, but I also felt the solace of what I would call the power of love. Because Rollie and I loved each other. It was no one's to take, it couldn't be stopped, no matter what.

Eventually my parents let Rollie back in. We promised not to have sex anymore, a promise we never intended to keep. I think everyone knew this. And from age fifteen to nineteen, I loved Rollie Carlson, and he loved me, and the world was safe and good and promising.

Me and Rollie, prom night, 1972

There was a custom at Carbondale Community High School whereby a junior or senior girl would be paired with a freshman girl to mentor her for her first year. The older girls were called Big Sisters. Mine turned out to be Anna Baker, the real big sister of one of my best friends, Mandy. Anna was the stuff of prom queen and bohemia combined. She knew how to traverse both realms, was a total stunner, and for this we all looked up to her. Tall, tan, a body to die for, and a personality to match—irreverent, supremely confident, bigger than life, really. I was hers. The first thing she did, being a woman of solid priorities, was teach me how to smoke opium. I already knew how to smoke cigarettes, so this was not a leap. We sat on the shag rug in her parents' living room with her connection, Leah, whose dad traveled to Indonesia a lot, and I got high. I never did figure out if Leah's dad actually brought the opium over—it seemed logical and certainly exotic—or if it was the more likely scenario in which Leah herself procured it from someone in the rich 1970 drug land of our large university town. Either way it was fine stuff.

The Baker girls were also revered for their talent for high drama. We all participated in Speech Team, where one could compete by reading prose or acting out a scene in a play either solo or with partners. I myself did prose as well as a duet acting stint from Carson McCullers's *The Member of the Wedding,* in which I played Frankie. Mandy tried her hand, with much success, in a scene as both Stella Kowalski and Blanche DuBois from *A Streetcar Named Desire.* Her final lines, and I can vividly remember her impassioned and desperate delivery at age fifteen: "I let the place go! *I* let the place go? Where were *you*? In bed with your—Polack!" She won every time. Naturally this kind of thing leaked over into our everyday lives, and Mandy was quite proud when, after being picked up late by her gentleman caller, Scott, she coolly responded to his acknowledgment of his tardiness by snipping, "You are very observative."

Mandy wasn't the only one who was challenged grammatically. Our friend Liz, upon going on one of her first dates ever, was sure to tell the waiter she didn't want "scrotums" on her salad, when obviously she meant to say croutons. Liz was another one who could seamlessly ride the line between cheerleader and bad girl, even if being bad meant nothing more than sneaking cigarettes behind the back of her protective older brother, Steve. Only Liz could pull off smoking with elegance, though. She was the most feminine of all of us, petite and blond and buxom. It took her an hour to do her makeup and hair, which was naturally curly at a time when straight hair was the way to go. I was the total opposite of Liz, and this attracted us to each other. I didn't wear makeup at all and wouldn't have been a cheerleader if you'd paid me. Whereas Liz was prim and well mannered, I veered toward the crude and obscene. I farted and burped freely, talked about sex explicitly, and generally delighted in grossing her out. She disapproved but really couldn't tear herself away.

Jane was more on my level. We had a certain lack of sophistication. It was Jane and I who gave pet names to all our friends' breasts. Liz was "Modest Mounds" for obvious reasons. Mandy was "Baby Nips," Jane was "Smashed Bananas," I was "Airplane Nose," and our Vietnamese pal, Pat, was "The Good Earth." Jane had delightful sayings like "Oh, balls!" and "You ain't a-woofin', honey!" and called everyone "doll." She suffered no fools. Jane and I also had the corner on musical obsession. She didn't play an instrument—that role was reserved for Joanne and me—but Janey and I swooned over our idols, something Joanne was far too cool to do. It was Jane and I who took on the arduous task of recording our own James Taylor interview. We got out a cassette player and would record a question: "James, we heard that you woke up in the night screaming. . . ." Then we would cue up his response from one of his albums, and this particular answer was James singing "just a bad dream . . ." from "Blues Is Just a Bad Dream" on his first record. This was vinyl, remember, so it required a fair bit of work to drop the needle in the exact right place. Another one of our questions was, "James"—we loved this, just saying his name—"James, what are the lyrics to your new song?" We delighted in our clever answer, from the very end of "Blossom": "La laaa la la la la laaa la la la la la la, la la la LA LA LA."

On New Year's Eve, the older Bakers always went out, leaving us to fend for ourselves in that fabulous house. My folks were teetotalers, while the Bakers showcased a complete liquor cabinet and had their five-o'clock highballs every evening. Mandy's aforementioned Scott came over one New Year's Eve, having been drinking before he got there and with plans to go on drinking after he left. Before he left, though, he needed to puke in the downstairs bathroom, and I guess he wasn't particularly neat about it. This was news to us when Dennis, Mandy's father, got home in his cups and used the bathroom. His wife, Donna, was in tow, her wig turned halfway around her head, giving her a sort of Liberace–meets–Louise Jefferson effect. After seeing the mess downstairs, Dennis interrogated Mandy, who could think on her feet and blamed the dog. Dennis paused as we all held our breaths and finally said, "Mandy? Mandy? Did you give that dog scotch? You know he was raised on gin." God bless Dennis. He got sober the same year I did—1983.

With my guitar on one side of me and Rollie and my good friends on the other, I coasted through high school. These were some of the most wonderful, grounded times of my whole life. I made decent enough grades to get by, although I recall precious little of what I learned in school, save for how to write a check and how to type. From Larry English I learned the words "twat" and "snatch." From Todd Stephens I found out what a great friend a guy can be. Oh, and I remember learning about tectonic plates and that flushing the toilet wastes water. Overall, life was simple and full. After I graduated from CCHS, though, things weren't so clear anymore.

5
Small Repairs

Eighteen years old, 1974

I wasn't born, I got spat out on a wall,
And nobody knew my name.
The sun hatched me out, cradle and all,
On the corner of First and Insane.

I couldn't wait to get out of The House. I took summer school for two summers straight in order to graduate from CCHS a year earlier than my friends, to graduate in Rollie's class. We had a fantasy of living on a remote shore in Australia after he got a degree in marine biology, and attending SIU together was a good start. In 1973, at the age of seventeen, I packed myself up and flew the coop with Rollie to the Thompson Point dorms, which were all of maybe three miles from Norwood Drive.

It was kind of a case of the emperor's new clothes. I was hell-bent for leather on becoming independent, but I really didn't have a clue about what to do next. The only reason I attended college at all was spite—I'd been told so many times by my high-school teachers how hard college would be that I had to prove a point, I suppose. I took refuge in required freshman courses like earth science and algebra, and as far as I could tell, they weren't any different from high-school classes except that they were way bigger and the teachers gave less of a damn.

One of my electives was modern dance. Don't ask me why, because I'm one of the least graceful people on the planet, and our first assignment was to make up a solo piece about something we did in our everyday lives. I painfully recall trying to "be" a shower; let's just leave it at that. Truly, I was a buffoon with regard to the whole undertaking of SIU, now that I had a choice in the matter. I had absolutely zero interest in studying anything that I can now, in hindsight, imagine I might have enjoyed. Music theory, no thanks. Philosophy, poetry, religion, art history, even the drama department didn't feel right, and here's the reason: My sense of balance was built on pretty thin ice, and without the confines of home, which afforded me something to rebel against, I was lost and extremely insecure. I'd never thought realistically about my vocation—it seemed to me that the world of academia, so revered by my family (my father had his Ph.D. by then, and Geoff was at Harvard on scholarship), was a drag, and I just always figured I'd do something "fun" like acting or painting or singing. Well, I was a mediocre actress and an even worse artist.

However. I could sing. And where does one go to sing in a college town that likes to party? Right down to Illinois Avenue, the "strip," to any dive that would hire me. My first official paying gig was at a bar called the American Tap, an old house converted into a bar. Colonial decor. For thirty dollars I played four forty-five-minute sets consisting of songs by Joni Mitchell, Paul Simon, James Taylor, Carole King, Bonnie Raitt, Judy Collins, CSN&Y, Jackson Browne, Judee Sill, and, of course, the Beatles. I loved it. I felt like I was doing what I was meant to do. I entered my sophomore year at SIU but rarely attended class. Too embarrassed to drop out formally, I just let it go.

Either I was playing somewhere or I was sitting in with someone else who was, more often than not, getting drunk in the process. I let Rollie go, too, and started dating a local musician named Jimmy Bruno. We lived the nightlife, closing down the bars and heading to whatever party ensued after that. Then we'd end up at Denny's for a predawn patty melt to soak up all the beer we'd consumed. With the money I was making, I bought a turquoise-and-coral bracelet, a pattern that continues to this day—I love jewelry and clothes and shoes. I may have mentioned that my mother is partially to blame. I share her love of fashion but, alas, not her sense of frugality. I make the money, I spend the money. I have a wardrobe my daughter envies, which is just as well, since it will constitute the bulk of her inheritance.

I started attracting a local following and thought I was hot stuff. We had a strong music community in Carbondale, and as I got better, I performed at other clubs in town. There was Gatsby's, a basement joint next to a pool hall whose owner sported a bad comb-over. Gatsby's had a proper stage, free popcorn, and the coldest draft beer in town. Up the street a couple of blocks was Das Fass, a German beer house of sorts, decorated with steins and wooden kegs. Das Fass had an outdoor stage, an indoor stage, and a downstairs room that resembled a bunker, where I played solo for a while, until I got the bug for company and more sound.

I decided to broaden my horizons and add more players to my little scene. Jimmy could play the bass, and he'd made friends with a drummer named Dennis Conroy who had been in a group called the Cryin' Shames. Dennis also played the tablas, which are hand drums originally from India. Let me just say right here that tablas are a bad idea. They have a distinct ring when played, and the ring can and needs to be tuned for each song key, which requires the pounding, up or down, of small wooden blocks on the side of the drum to adjust the tone. And Dennis was a perfectionist. Who would ever have thought that endless amounts of time could be spent between songs waiting for the drummer to tune? I took a major leap and went electric, hiring Jim's friend Jack O'Boyle on lead guitar, which ultimately meant putting Dennis on a real drum kit, effectively ending the infernal tuning of the tablas. We were the Shawn Colvin Band. Rock 'n' roll!

Shawn Colvin Band—Jack O'Boyle, me, Dennis Conroy,
and Brian Sandstrom—SIU campus, 1975

Our repertoire consisted of the same material I'd done by myself, with the addition of some Bob Marley, a few of Jim's songs, and a lot of the new incarnation of Fleetwood Mac. At this point wardrobe was becoming key, and between Joni Mitchell and Stevie Nicks I was getting my look down. One New Year's Eve, I was booked to play Das Fass, and all I could think about was what to wear. On the cover of *For the Roses* by Joni Mitchell, which had come out a few years back, she was wearing a green velvet tunic with matching green velvet pants that were tucked into a pair of tall, blond Frye boots. I managed to find the boots, but the velvet situation was more challenging. Being Barb Colvin's daughter, I had some sewing chops and went on down to Fashion Fabrics, where the only green velvet available was a bright Kelly green, not at all like Joni's sage green outfit. What to do? I went with brown, deciding that Joni's vibe on *For the Roses* was decidedly organic, donned the boots, and was set.

All decked out, I went to do my gig, and between the first and second sets I got so drunk I actually could not play. This had never happened before. Looking back now, I can see it's clear that my behavior was certainly alcoholic in nature, although I wouldn't be able to make that determination for another ten years.

Although I'd had anxiety my whole life, I'd always found ways to manage it, but I was at an age, nineteen, when, biologically, depression can really kick in. And although I felt at home onstage, emotionally I was starting to unravel. Drinking wasn't enough to keep me grounded. Neither was singing or my guitar at the foot of the bed. For one thing, making a living as a musician was just not done as far as I could tell. I knew lots of people, including my parents, who loved music and had talent for it, but none of them made it a profession except for the father of my childhood friend Ruth, who was our church organist in Vermillion. I was pretty sure I wasn't going that route, but I didn't know where I *was* going. I felt fraudulent.

That summer I'd been smoking a lot of pot, almost daily, which was just nasty stuff for me. It made me trippy and paranoid, but my older and therefore wiser boyfriend, Jim, was big on it, so we smoked. One night in August 1975, we got stoned and saw *Nashville,* a quintessential Robert Altman movie in which the heroine, a famous singer played by Ronee Blakley, gets shot. If pot makes you trippy, you most likely don't want to be smoking and going to one of the typical seventies-era Altman films, brilliant though they may be, and this is particularly true if the singer heroine gets shot and you have visions of yourself as a singer heroine. When we left the theater, I was suddenly overwhelmed with the most pervasive sense of doom and terror. In an effort to feel safe, I made Jim take me to my parents' house. But they didn't know what was wrong either.

That attack subsided, but never completely, and I had the nearly constant feeling during the next few months that something terrible was going to happen, a visceral sense that even the ground I was walking on wasn't to be trusted as stable. At times the panic would begin to rise and I'd have to leave wherever I was and run outside to breathe.

The bottom completely fell out that October when I happened to see a TV show about John Kennedy and the Bay of Pigs, called *The Missiles of October.* All that free-floating terror got sucked into a vortex of concentrated, specific horror: nuclear war. I became sure it was imminent. I couldn't eat or sleep, and I saw signs of the impending holocaust everywhere. For example, at that time a Simon & Garfunkel song called "My Little Town" was quite popular, and there was a lyric in it that repeated over and over: "Nothing but the dead and dying / Back in my little town." One morning I turned on the radio and those were the words I heard. I was sure it was a sign. It's one of the things that can happen when the brain chemistry goes hinky, and extreme anxiety is often a component of depression. My brain can get stuck, and terrible, catastrophic thoughts loop around in my head, rooting me to the spot, waves of icy terror shooting down my limbs.

My parents tried their best to comfort me. I was extremely needy. I would call on them at all hours, when I felt like I was just going to lose my mind. At any given time—and it was fairly constant by this point—the terror was paralyzing. Their house felt like the safest place I could be. If I could get there, I could take up residence on the family-room couch, where I would sit for hours, but I couldn't always get to their house. I recall being at my apartment once, and I was unable to get from my room to my car. I was too scared. I called home, and my dad answered. There weren't any cell phones then—can you imagine? I mean, the last time I went to the ER, I took an ambulance and texted my friend Robin the entire time. (As I grew older, I learned to take my panic when necessary to the ER, but when I was nineteen, my parents *were* the ER.) I called my father, and he walked me theoretically out of the kitchen and to the front door. The plan was to get to the car just outside. We hung up. I got stuck in the kitchen. I couldn't move. I didn't understand how. I called back. This time I actually walked to the front door, but I had to walk back into the kitchen to hang up. I got stuck again. I called back. I remember talking to him and staring at my stacks of record albums on the shelves, the comfort of music a distant memory.

What the hell was going on? No one knew. I felt hideous. I couldn't eat. I couldn't sleep. I was immobilized. Finally my parents took me to a psychiatrist, who first killed the anxiety with a tranquilizer so rad that I didn't care if the world blew up right then and there. Next he started me on Elavil, an antidepressant in the tricyclic family that is now old-school, but I'll be damned if it didn't work *exactly* in the time predicted—three weeks. Three weeks that I spent getting blurred vision and dry mouth and listening constantly to *The Hissing of Summer Lawns,* Joni Mitchell's new record. It was 1975. One morning I woke up and the dread was gone. Gone. I was better.

I should have stayed on medication from then on, but one of the frustrating things about depressed people—and there are many, lest you think we don't know—is that feeling better tends to convince us that there was nothing wrong in the first place. Like childbirth—you forget. But it's unlike childbirth in that you want to deny that anything ever happened, so after a few months I stopped taking the Elavil with seemingly little consequence, but as I look back at the ensuing years of alcoholism, it seems likely that I was, at least in part, just trying to medicate the depression.

My confidence was badly shaken by what was really my first mental breakdown, and whatever had gone wrong neurochemically was to be my shadow from then on—sometimes worse, sometimes better. We didn't call it depression; we didn't know what to call it. I was barely nineteen, but already my mood disorder was such that I was a slave to it, and although my band was gaining some momentum, it felt to me like a burden.

We were getting bookings up in Champaign-Urbana and Chicago. I convinced my father to cosign a loan and bought a sound system and a van. By the time we'd taken just two trips in that van, I was ready to sell it to the guitar player. The trips made me horribly anxious, and I was overwhelmed by my responsibilities as bandleader, which entailed booking the gigs, making the travel arrangements, and keeping track of the accounting. A mere six months after I'd started the Shawn Colvin Band, I disbanded it.

In addition to everything else, I'd basically blown out my voice trying to sing rock and roll. I'm not a rock singer; this much I've learned. I can't wail. I wish to God I could. I love rock and roll and blues and soul. I can sing country and folk, and it took me years to realize that I was the quintessential lass with the acoustic guitar meant to be warbling romantic sonnets.

I was told I had nodules on my vocal cords, which are basically calluses. The cords can't vibrate together properly anymore; the nodes get in the way, and too much air is forced through, making the voice sound hoarse. There are two options for treatment—vocal rest or surgery—and I couldn't face either one. The Dixie Diesels were a Carbondale country-swing outfit à la Asleep at the Wheel, but they were short a girl singer, and their new fiddle player, Willy Wainwright, was short a girlfriend. Bingo. I snagged myself a boyfriend and a band in one fell swoop, abandoning my own band, retreating instead to the relative safety of the Diesels, where someone else was in charge and I didn't have to sing as much. Then the Dixie Diesels decided that in order to make it, they'd have to move. To Austin. What the hell. If I was ever going to get out of Carbondale, this was my shot.

6
Walking on a Wire

The Dixie Diesels—Brad Davis, Charlie Morrill, Radar Hurst,
Mike Potter, me, and Willy Wainwright—1976

I go to the trouble like a magnet.
That's where I'll be.
Trouble is just a place to sing.
It's what you need.

Austin was a revelation. I expected Texas to be flat and dry, like the movie *Giant*, but Austin is hilly and green and lush and lovely. You know how some places just feel good, something about the smell of the air and the nature of the light? Austin is like that. Willy had lived in Austin before and couldn't wait to show me around. Our first night there, we went to the now-defunct Armadillo World Headquarters, a terrific music venue, where we saw Ry Cooder and I was introduced to nachos with jalapeño slices, something Willy insisted was a necessary initiation. We stayed that first night in the still-thriving Austin Motel on South Congress Street, whose marquee usually boasts the slogan "So Close Yet So Far Out." The Dixie Diesels consisted of me on vocals and acoustic guitar, Willy on fiddle, Mike Potter on bass, Brad Davis on vocals and rhythm guitar, Rusty "Radar" Hurst on lead guitar and pedal steel, and Charlie Morrill on drums. Radar was so named because he looked exactly like the character in *M*A*S*H*.

Our regular gig in Austin was at the Split Rail on South Lamar, a total dive with an asphalt floor, loved by all, a major hangout. Everybody went—hippies, conservatives, radicals, politicians. We all danced and sang and got drunk together on Shiner beer, gathering at wooden tables that had been carved up over the years.

I sang a fair bit of Patsy Cline, Willie Nelson, some of Chris O'Connell's songs from Asleep at the Wheel, like "Space Buggy," and a whole lot of Emmylou Harris, whom I adore. It was my boyfriend, Willy, who introduced me to Emmylou via Gram Parsons. Our band did everything from Merle Haggard to duets between Radar and Willy by Stéphane Grappelli and Django Reinhardt, and some originals thrown in, too, like Brad's "My Car Has a Mind of Its Own," a song about drinking. I'd say most of the material we did was about drinking.

The group didn't play just in Austin. I spent nearly two years on the road with the Diesels doing a circuit of dance halls all over the Southwest, where the two-step, the Cotton-Eyed Joe, and the schottische were the order of the night. We'd head over to West Texas and El Paso, into Santa Fe, then up through Evergreen, Colorado, and back to Austin. I remember our having pet names for one another in the Diesels based on the nature of our farts. Brad, for example, was "Seepage," his famous line being, "Was it me? I don't know!" It was all scatological good fun, and such is the stuff of living in vans with guys.

Our gigs generally lasted for about four or five hours, and we had to do "Orange Blossom Special," a fiddle instrumental that got faster and faster, like a runaway train, inciting the dancers to go absolutely mental. Timing was crucial with the "Orange Blossom Special," and we played it at the end of about the third set. If it were played any later, people would be too drunk and fall over. Sometimes they fell over anyway.

Not only was I given a major tutorial in country and swing music in Austin, I got to hear a whole passel of great Texas songwriters like Butch Hancock, Gary P. Nunn, Willis Alan Ramsey, Joe Ely, Guy Clark, Townes Van Zandt, Jimmie Dale Gilmore, and Uncle Walt's Band with Walter Hyatt, Champ Hood, and David Ball. I still do a song by Uncle Walt's Band, called "Don't You Think I Feel It Too," taught to me by my friends Paul Glasse and Gary Hartman,

We stayed in rank hotels and on people's floors and paid ourselves twenty-five dollars a night. The rest was for gas, van maintenance, hotels, and travel expenses. We drank too much beer and ate too many burgers and pieces of pie in greasy truck stops. I miss it all. Once when we were in Evergreen, I stopped in a store and bought a pair of Levi's 501s, the good kind, when they were still shrink-to-fit and felt like cardboard until you washed them. I remember that day and the smell of pine and warm morning sun and the satisfied feeling of being carefree in the mountains and on the road and getting a new pair of jeans. I still have the jeans and have put them in a trunk for my daughter.

The Dixie Diesels had such an influence on me. I would eventually settle in Austin. I learned scads about great music I'd never been exposed to before. I met a man named Buddy Miller in Austin, and he would reappear in my life down the line and ultimately change it. But after two years of hard road work, the Diesels hadn't really gotten any further than eking out a living, and my voice, while improved, wasn't really getting better. I still had nodes, and I was going to have to do something about them. The thing was, I just thought I'd always be able to sing. There wasn't really any space between who I was and the fact that I sang; they were one and the same. My vocal range was getting whittled down to just a few notes, barely an octave, and I'd always thought I could sing anything. Now that notion was toast, and that's where more trouble began.

I decided to stop singing. I signed up for speech therapy and got a job as a salesgirl at a boutique in Austin called the Bizarre, the place to go if you needed edible undies. Willy stayed with the band and kept touring. I now lived alone for all intents and purposes, for the first time in my life, and wouldn't you know I didn't have the first idea how to do it. The main problem was feeding myself. I've never been any good at cooking (ask both my ex-husbands), and I was so used to eating with Willy that I couldn't figure out how to cook for just me. And I was lonely. And bored. So two things happened: I took up running, and I ate less.

I was lean anyway, and young, and before long I looked like Frank Shorter. I liked it. As I lost weight, I noticed that clothes looked better on me, more like the way they looked on models in magazines. I had body issues, of course. If you grow up female in our culture, you just do. For whatever reason, "it" took hold of me. I became obsessed with losing weight, with buying smaller clothes. I stopped at the local supermarket every day, because they had one of those large scales you could put a nickel in and weigh yourself. I was 115. I was 110. I was 105. And so on.

Anorexic 1978—Kay, me, Clay, and Grandpa Colvin

A girlfriend of mine diagnosed me right off the bat when I told her I had counted the number of peas I ate at Luby's Cafeteria. "Oooooh, anorexia!" she said, but I didn't care. With no singing to give me identity, this newfound talent for becoming thinner took over. Nothing was more important. The more I lost, the better. I felt supremely in control, but really I was losing it, figuratively and literally. I lost the job at the Bizarre and a couple of other jobs after that. I would binge-eat and -drink once a week or so and then not show up for work out of remorse.

I returned to Carbondale and moved back in with my parents, with the idea that I would study fashion. The truth is, I couldn't take care of myself. I had failed at living away and alone and needed to go home, but an academic plan sounded so much better. And I probably I wanted someone to see I was sick. But you couldn't tell me anything. You couldn't make me eat.

Breakfast was half a container of yogurt. Lunch was an apple. Dinner was a broiled skinless chicken breast and a tomato. My mother made that for me every night, because I would eat it. As we sat down at the dining-room table, my mom and dad at either end, my sister and brother on one side, and me on the other, they would all tuck into their lasagna or pot roast while I picked at my pathetic little meal.

I rode my bicycle to school, jumped rope, and ran. My favorite class was tailoring, because we had to make a suit precisely fitted to our own body, down to the last inch. Mine looked like a little boy's outfit. I bottomed out at eighty-six pounds. Minor cuts wouldn't heal. My hair was falling out. I don't know how I beat it, I really don't. I like to say I was hungry, unlike a lot of anorexics, and that was a big part of it. I was hungry and all I did was think about food.

Fortunately, my parents found me a psychiatrist, an infinitely kind man named Anthony Berger, who assured me from the start that he would not try to take my thinness away from me, that he knew it was too important. I have no idea if anyone was thinking of hospitalizing me.

The whole episode lasted about a year. I don't know why I was so lucky that it didn't last my whole life. The major crisis passed, and I was no longer starving, although whatever issues were underneath the anorexia weren't really dealt with. I began to think about singing again, and I suspect that was the ticket. My voice had healed, although it was quite weak, and I got a couple of gigs around town. I began to eat. And eat. I made up for lost time. At any given sitting, I could consume an entire box of cornflakes, an entire large pizza (Quatro's, the best deep-dish in Carbondale), a half gallon of cheap ice cream, or a loaf of cracked-wheat bread, toasted, with butter. A six-pack of beer was not a stretch either. And this is when I fell in love with alcohol, really and truly. So, basically, I traded one problem for another.

At a bar with Mom and Dad, 1978

I gained sixty pounds in three months and looked like a whale. I was twenty-two and fat and drunk and living with my parents, a far cry from the girl who just a few years back had seemed so full of promise. To top it all off, I got a job taking care of rats in the university vivarium—the place where they kept animals for experimentation. I needed money to get myself out of town to go somewhere, anywhere. I would wake up in the morning and put on the only things that fit—a pair of ratty sweatpants and my dad's T-shirt, and head out to clean up rodent shit. It was a low point, to be sure. But something was coming alive in me, because I would sneak off from rat duty and write little tidbits of lyrics. These weren't the musings of a teenager attempting to imitate a hero. I had grown up a bit and had something to say about it.

> *No one ever said it was easy.*
> *I've always been along for the ride,*
> *Thinking there would always be*
> *Someone to take the wheel for me,*
> *But I was helpless sitting passenger side . . .*

Not exactly brilliant, but it was *me* speaking, reflecting, trying to get at something. It was new. But it would be many years before I started to believe I could really write.

7
Out There on Her Own

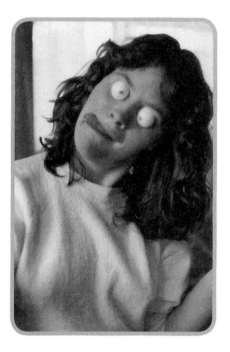

Like I said, fat and drunk, 1979

I am weaving like a drunkard, like a balloon up in the air.
I am needing a puncture and someone to point me somewhere.

Having cleaned up enough rat shit to last a lifetime, I finally had enough money saved to try leaving home again. This was the real thing, do or die. My old boyfriend, Jim Bruno, had moved to Berkeley and loved it. Armed with my guitar, my protective layer of fat, and a daily ration of alcohol, I headed out for the San Francisco Bay area in the spring of 1979.

I moved into a large, rambling, run-down house in Berkeley with Jimmy and a few other misfits, in an attic room with a skylight. Many were the nights that I drank a six-pack of Coors and crawled out onto the roof from where I could see out across the bay to the lights of San Francisco. I remember precious little about my yearlong stint in the Bay Area, because I was drunk most of the time. I call it my lost weekend.

Most of my roommates were Deadheads. They didn't drink Coors; they ate watermelon laced with acid. Let me say right now, with all apologies, that I never dialed in the Grateful Dead. You either get it or you don't, and I am not among the converted. To me my roommates were what I imagined vintage San Franciscans to be, all Haight-Ashbury and free love and you better wear some flowers in your hair. One morning I was in the kitchen and one of my roommates, Julie, a lanky, wire-rimmed, long-stringy-haired, peasant-skirted, pit-hair-baring, sandal-wearing gal, stumbled in. As I was pouring myself a glass of orange juice, she said, "Hey, man, can I have a hit of your smoothie?"—assuming, naturally, that it was spiked with something.

The first order of business was getting a job, naturally, but that took some time, and in the interim I developed a ritual. After recovering from my morning hangover, I would scan the classifieds and make feeble attempts toward employment. Then something divine happened.

The documentary about the Who, *The Kids Are Alright,* came to the local cinema. I went to see it one afternoon and fell head over heels in love with the band. My musical leanings had veered from a well-balanced overview, and due to my unbending allegiance to the Beatles I ignored what I thought to be lesser bands like the Stones, the Kinks, Led Zeppelin, and the Who, among others. I went again the next day. And the next, and the next. Some days I just sat in the theater waiting for the next show and saw it twice. I have no idea how many times I saw that movie but it was *a lot.*

At night when I was going to sleep, I fantasized about meeting them, just as I'd done with the Fab Four when I was nine. I was twenty-three! Never mind. I was in love. Yes, of course I'd seen Woodstock, but I'd passed over them in favor of Crosby, Stills & Nash and Joan Baez. Now I finally got it. Only four guys and three instruments. One guitar player—and what a guitar player. Pete, Pete, Pete. There he was in his white jumpsuit, lovingly bent over his ax with bloody fingers, or windmilling and leaping for all he was worth, like a punk ballerina. Oh, I wanted to be him. Let's not even mention his songwriting. The mind boggles. And of course Roger, god of six-pack abs and mike-whirling finesse; the stoic, solid John Entwistle on bass; and the one-in-a-million carnival ride of a drummer, Keith Moon. But finally the sad day came when I got a job, and my secret afternoons with *The Kids Are Alright* had to end.

I was hired by a stained-glass store in Oakland as a salesperson. I learned how to cut and handle glass, but not without a few minor accidents that put me closer to emulating dear Pete at his bloody best. I made fast friends with a woman named Shelley Arrowwood. She was amused by the way I put down our insane boss and decided that *this* kid was all right.

Shelley had taken on her last name when she grew tired of changing it every time she got married, which was fairly often, so she legally became "Arrowwood," nature lover to the core, for good and always. I called her "Arrowhead," and she called me "Shufflefoot McQueen"—I'm not sure why, although I think it had something to do with the fact that I shuffled like a downtrodden subordinate every time our drill-sergeant boss commanded me to make coffee, muttering under my breath as I inched toward the coffeemaker.

We had a quick, easy, shorthand of a friendship, and I spent lots of time with her and her then-spouse, Richard. Shelley was a football-loving, hard-drinking, foul-mouthed little thing, and Richard was a refined and professorial die-hard feminist. One night as we were watching TV, an ad came on for what was then a revolutionary development in sanitary napkins—the three adhesive strips. Richard took this in and suddenly erupted in outrage. "Jesus! Look at what they put you through! This is unbelievable!" Shelley and I stared at him blankly for a minute until we finally understood—Richard, in his hypervigilance to root out the atrocities done to women, was under the impression that one took the sticky part of the pad and applied it directly to the crotch. Ouch.

Shelley

Musically I was keeping things strictly acoustic—no more bands for me—and found a home at Laval's Subterranean in Berkeley, yet another basement bar. Jim was still writing songs, and I was finally getting a clue that doing original music might be a good idea. I did a lot of his tunes, plus material by Tom Waits, Bruce Springsteen, and Bob Dylan. Covering songs by men was a good trick I had discovered—sometimes the simple fact that a woman was singing the song would give it another dimension. It was during this period that I taught myself to play "The Heart of Saturday Night" by Waits and "You're Gonna Make Me Lonesome When You Go" by Dylan. For the first time, I felt that there was something special going on with my interpretations, and ultimately both those songs made it onto my third record, *Cover Girl.*

Me and Jim Bruno, Berkeley, 1979

Although I still didn't write my own songs, it's worth noting that I was always fooling around on the guitar, and from time to time I would compose little ideas here and there:

> *I've been sleeping fair,*
> *Lately I could swear I'm thinking*
> *Clearer and clearer,*
> *And I've been working hard,*
> *Looking at my punch card and*
> *My mirror, my mirror . . .*

I went back to this tidbit years later and finished it, called it "Ricochet in Time," and included it on my first record, *Steady On.* It's a song I still love to perform, because it describes being a musician on the road. In fact, it means a lot more to me now than it did when I wrote it.

I don't know how long I might have stayed in the Bay Area, but a year after I moved there, fate intervened when I got a phone call that set the wheels in motion to significantly change the rest of my life, both personally and professionally. The Big Apple beckoned.

8
Dry Is Good

The Buddy Miller Band—Karl Himmel, Buddy, me,
Larry Campbell, and Lincoln Schleifer—NYC, 1980

You're shining, I can see you.
You're smiling. That's enough.
I'm holding on to you
Like a diamond in the rough.

New York City, just like I pictured it. I had visited there exactly once, and it had made me dizzy with its immensity. I would never have possessed the nerve to move to Manhattan without a single connection, but Buddy Miller tracked me down in California and asked if I would join his band. I knew Buddy from my days in Austin, and he'd gone up to New York to hop onto the bandwagon of what became known as the great country scare of the 1980s, what with urban cowboys, Gilley's, electric-bull riding, and two-stepping. All the things I'd already seen and heard in Austin were now trendy in New York, and Bud went there to see what could be done about enlightening the Yankees to a bit of homegrown, honestly-come-by, grassroots, serious-assed country music. Never mind that Buddy was a Jew from New Jersey. God didn't get the right memo about Bud.

I was to replace Julie Griffin, one of the deepest, purest singers and songwriters ever. She was Buddy's girlfriend at the time (and is now his wife) but had had enough of bars and bands and brawls and vans and boys and smoke and sawdust and beer, and she went back home to Texas. I accepted the job and moved to New York in November of 1980.

Buddy must have been really bereft when Julie left the band. After all, he left to join her less than a year later. He never showed it, though. Our band was close, but we didn't confide in each other. Our private lives were private, or as private as they could be while we were living out of a van together. I knew that Bud liked Chinese-Cuban food and had the most extensive record collection of any of us. I knew he could sing and play the guitar like a maniac, there being a complete disconnect between this gentle soul and this ferocious player.

I saw Bud now and then over the years after he left New York. He and Julie came to visit and showed up at my gig at the Lone Star Cafe. Buddy managed to record my set off the board and still talks about it. That's Bud, the archivist. He joined Emmylou Harris's band, and I happened to see him in Memphis around 1995 while both Emmy and I were there. Over the breakfast table, he took out a bootleg CD and pushed it across the table to me. "Listen to this," he said, and I looked at the disc. Patty Griffin. It was the first album she'd recorded with a producer, and it never saw the light of day, but upon first listen I was completely blown away. And now I'm in a band called Three Girls and Their Buddy, with Emmy, Patty, and Buddy. This is evidence of good karma, surely.

How do I explain Buddy Miller? He is made of music. He is made of light. He's like your best big brother and your sweetest child. There is no one kinder. He once gave me a book called *How to Torture Your Children*. It was Buddy who recently turned me on to *Some Kind of Monster,* the Metallica documentary. On tour he gifted us with plush monkey toys that flew and screamed. He reveals little about himself but steps up to the plate as a producer, something I'm about to be witness to, since he's going to produce my next record. Buddy and Patty just won a Grammy for the gospel record he produced for her. Bud has religion, but he doesn't preach it, he lives it.

We almost lost Bud in 2009. Three Girls and Their Buddy were touring. In Baltimore, Buddy confessed after a show to having acute indigestion, but Carolyn, our tour manager, thought it was more than that. She carted him off to the Johns Hopkins ER, where it was determined he was having not acute indigestion but a massive heart attack. He was stabilized—only barely, though. By early the next morning, the surgeons opened him up and performed a triple bypass. It's notable that instead of having three major arteries going into his heart, as most people do, Buddy possesses four. He has a special heart. This fourth artery was not completely blocked, and it, along with

Carolyn and Johns Hopkins, saved his life. It's a good thing, too, because once God *did* get the memo on Buddy, I can assure you he broke the mold.

But back to 1980. The Buddy Miller Band consisted of its namesake, myself, Lincoln Schleifer on bass, Karl Himmel on drums, and Larry Campbell on everything—guitar, pedal steel, fiddle, and mandolin. Years later, when the movie *Dances with Wolves* came out, Larry's wife dubbed him "Walks with Instruments." Buddy found Karl in Nashville, I believe, and knew of his work with Neil Young. Larry and Lincoln were young New York City boys ripe for the picking, and Buddy sniffed them out somehow. I have been in a lot of vans with boys and should know more than I woefully do about how men operate. I recall things like the time Lincoln was snoring in the backseat. I tape-recorded him and called the piece "Mammals of the Bronx." The only thing I can say with certainty is that given enough time and alcohol, most of them tried to sleep with me.

We played several pseudo–country joints in the city, most notably City Limits on Seventh Avenue. I remember other places, like Home and Spaghetti Western, but our main haunts were City Limits, and the Lone Star Cafe. Buddy's band also played a circuit of bars up through New Paltz and Albany, New York, hazardous undertakings given that we all drank. On Larry's birthday, in fact, between sets we were all downing kamikazes, which consist of equal parts vodka, triple sec, and lime juice, and in an effort to be one of the guys I confidently offered to drive us all back to the city. At some point during that drive, I lost consciousness, I guess for only a second or so, because when I came to, we were still on the road.

I wish I could remember a set list from Buddy's band. I was so drunk. Bud picked out a song for me called "Runnin' Wild," and he and I did a duet called "Rock, Salt, and Nails" that he'd done first with Julie and would later record with her. Larry turned me on to a song by his friend Roly Salley, called "Killin' the Blues." I did that one, too. And, of course, the "Orange Blossom Special." Buddy used to call out the set list to us, song by song. He decided on the fly what to play, and he always needed to tell us what key the next song was in—we knew so many that the rest of us would forget, although he never did. Always he would announce each song to us like this: "Okay, 'Silver Wings' in the key of G . . . like a little baby goat." Or " 'Six Days on the Road' in E . . . like a tiny egg."

After mooching off each band member for a place to stay over the course of a few weeks, I finally found an apartment in the East Village, a true shithole for two hundred dollars a month on East Third Street between First and Second avenues, known as the Hells Angels block. I was ecstatic to get it. It was a studio in a six-floor walk-up with crumbling plaster, rotting linoleum, a bathtub in the kitchen, sporting the luxury of its own toilet in a little cubicle near the tub. The ceiling literally fell from that cubicle one day and made a nice pile of plaster and drywall inside the toilet bowl, upon which, luckily, I was not sitting at that moment. The apartment was too hot in the summer, too cold in the winter. Water was leaking from the ceiling into my room one day, and I discovered, after knocking on his door, that the guy above me was a hoarder and had stacks of newspapers four feet high everywhere. He had no idea his radiator was leaking, because it was practically impossible to see, let alone get to.

East Third Street, 1981

I fell in love with New York. The geeky, neurotic weirdo I'd always felt like began to seem downright normal compared to some of the things I witnessed every day! And I loved the feeling that no matter the time of day or night, New York City was open. The Bay Area always felt too spread out for me to get a grip on, but New York was laid out on a simple grid that made it feel small. No matter what I needed, it was just around the corner. There were the Ukrainian diners where I'd buy a quart of split-pea soup and a loaf of pumpernickel bread and live off that for a week, and the electronics store on the corner was where I bought my first television, a thirteen-inch black-and-white. I didn't have to sweat not having a car; the subway was all I needed.

And I met Stokes.

He just showed up at one of my gigs. I think it was at the Other End. I know there was an introduction, but I don't remember it. He wasn't in my life, and then one day he was. Roy Stokes Howell. He was called Stokes. He could talk to anybody about anything. You meet Stokes and he already knows you. Then the next time you see him, you just say, "Well it's Stokes, of course," and there you are. He's your friend.

Stokes and I are kind of the same person, except that he likes for rooms to be hot and I like them to be cold. We are both attracted to insanely wrong lovers for ourselves. In some way, shape, or form, we contemplate suicide daily. We think *Waiting for Godot* is one of the funniest things ever written. We would be lost without fart and shit humor. I watched *Silence of the Lambs* like five times, and Stokes accused me of being sick, but he watched *Blue Velvet* at *least* five times. He also reads a lot of books about serial killers and shark attacks. We love the line from *Shadow of a Doubt* where Joseph Cotten asks his innocent young niece, "Do you know the world is a foul sty?" This means a lot to us. We not only like but can also *relate* to the film *Repulsion*. We love *Huckleberry Finn*.

Stokes grew up in Missouri; he's a small-town boy. I grew up in South Dakota. Small-town girl. We both became New Yorkers so as not to be seen as strange anymore. We were *Romper Room* compared to most of our neighbors in the East Village. Stokes studies Buddhism. Buddhists really do believe that the world is a foul sty, but Stokes and I come by that point of view naturally; it's in our bones. We are both kind, honest friends, dedicated and passionate and open in our work. In fact, Stokes, a writer, is so open in his work that one of his friends declared his first book of short stories "a cry for help." You would want us on your jury if you did it but didn't mean to. We understand. He lived practically just around the corner, on Sixth Street between Avenue A and First Avenue.

Stokes nursed me through months of torment—hell, maybe years—with my first real adult boyfriend, John Leventhal, staying on the phone with me for hours. He drove a cab during the day and stayed up all night writing. So if the panic attacks came in the middle of the night, I would hightail it over to East Sixth, where he would have a small paper bag ready for me to breathe into to stop the hyperventilating. That's love. Then he'd let me sleep in his bed until early morning, his bedtime.

After I stopped drinking, Stokes was at the ready to handle the strange fallout from the void. I remember days when I would robotically go downstairs to the corner deli and buy one Diet Pepsi at a time, drink it and chain-smoke, toss the can in the trash, and head back down for another. Back and forth. I was like Paula Prentiss in *The Stepford Wives* after she gets stabbed in the gut by Katharine Ross and her mechanics go haywire, causing her to retrieve teacups from the cupboard again and again. Turn, drop them, go back, turn, drop, all the while repeating, "Oh Joanna! My new dress! How could you do a thing like that? Just when I was going to give you coffee! How could you do a thing like that? I thought we were friends!" Nobody stabbed me, but my machinery was broken and had switched to an out-of-order autopilot. By putting his hand on my arm, Stokes could stop the loop, and then he would rub my shoulders. Human contact. I stopped. I felt. I wept. I needed a witness; it was too frightening otherwise. Stokes was one of my witnesses.

Nothing was too out there for Stokes and me to discuss, from sexual perversions and experiments gone awry to the lowest in fart and shit humor up to and including our own ghastly moments of scatological mishaps, my favorite being a bus ride Stokes once was on in Missouri. As he took a poo in the back restroom, he discovered the lock on the door to be broken and so had to hold it shut.

The bus then rounded a tight corner, launching poor Stokes out of his throne and into the aisle as if to wave a quick, pants-at-the-ankles hello before the bus turned in the other direction and set him back down on the toilet. And these weren't every now and then whispered and giggled confessions—this was dinner conversation. It still is.

Me and Stokes, NYC, 1983

What I loved about New York wasn't just having Stokes in the neighborhood. Even the music community seemed small and tight-knit. If our band didn't have a gig, we were usually out seeing someone else's, and it was totally copacetic to be in more than one band. Soozie Tyrell, who fronted a group called High in the Saddle, had a revolving door of girl backup singers that included Elaine Caswell, Lisa Lowell, Patti Scialfa, and me. We'd play in duos, trios, whatever got us hired, and Soozie was a master at sniffing out work. They all could sing anything—Elaine killed on Bacharach & David, Lisa wailed on Wanda Jackson, Patti channeled Ronnie Spector and Dusty Springfield, and Soozie—she played the hell out of the violin and sang absolutely everything with the most joyful, gigantic, shit-eating grin and a toss of her fiery red hair. Not only that, she hand-beaded bustiers for all of us girls in her spare time and could drink every one of us under the table.

Lisa Lowell, me, and Soozie Tyrell, City Limits, NYC, 1983

And we drank. Did I mention we drank? Well, I shouldn't speak for anyone else. No—no, on second thought I will. Given any provocation, from celebrating New Year's Eve to nursing a hangnail, one or all of us was bound to be completely shit-faced drunk.

9
Wind Is Better

You can sing Hallelujah,
You can fly like a bird,
You can cry like an angel
When there are no words.

Ah yes, the drinking. I myself was a cheap drunk—beer was fine—and a pleasant one, too. Also extremely consistent. Alcohol use? Check "daily." Basically I was self-medicating. While imbibing, I just got happy. But at some point after I moved to New York, I had to admit I had crossed that invisible line. I wasn't drinking because I chose to. I was drinking because I had to.

I found a Buddhist reading once that spoke of the eighty-four thousand different delusions. I even wrote a song about it, because it bent my brain. It refers to the idea that our very lives are just delusions, but I can't get my head around that. I worked too hard to fulfill this dream that so caters to my ego. The attention of an audience is still paramount to my well-being, and my only consolation is that the songs I write and the music I sing and play might move someone. I like the term "moves," because it indicates that one is actually taken from one place to another, a literal journey of the soul, and I believe that art can do this. There is a line in a song of mine—"If there were no music, then I would not get through"—and surely at my best I'm expressing something approaching purity of emotion. So perhaps there is hope beyond my base concept that ego alone drives me.

Certainly the most pointed delusions in my life have been my addictions, although there aren't quite eighty-four thousand of them. Close, though. I don't know how you get any more deluded, to succumb to something that tells you that as long as you use it, you will feel better, when in fact the whole cycle of getting high, coming down, and getting high again is a form of insanity and slow death. How does this happen? I've always thought it's the lethal combination of a general lack of maturity, specifically the inability to delay gratification, plus an inherited predisposition toward addiction in general and, in my case, a little clinical anxiety disorder and depression thrown in for good measure. It didn't help that I made my living in bars. I couldn't control my intake of anything. If having a few drinks or cigarettes or some cocaine was good, then more was absolutely better. (By the way, I never tried heroin, mushrooms, crack, meth, Ecstasy, speed, or anything else I can think of. . . . Oh, except opium.) Some of you know the drill: The morning after brings hangovers and feelings of self-loathing along with a physical withdrawal that's assuaged by more drugs, and invariably the cycle starts up all over again. I remember one night in particular when I had no plans—nothing to do, no one to see, and no place to go. It made sense to stay in and take a break from the party. I couldn't do it. I went to the downstairs deli, bought a six-pack of Budweiser, went back upstairs, and drank it all. Alone. This stands out because I remember being ashamed that I literally couldn't do without alcohol for twenty-four hours, and as far as I was concerned, I had no choice.

Drinking started out great back in college but quickly became a vicious circle of blessed inebriation and the inevitable aftermath.

The hangovers were deadly and probably turned out to be my salvation. I first felt suicidal when I was hungover, the effects of alcohol ultimately worsening the depression I was trying to keep at bay. In the midst of one crushing morning after, I realized that this is who I turned out to be—a drunk. I saw my future bleakly laid out before me, and I wanted to die.

I had a friend named Constance. We were drinking buddies. I remember watching a PBS show with her one Saturday morning while we both nursed brutal hangovers. The program was about gazelles and their proficiency for leaping, and we were quietly taking in the relative absurdity of watching a creature so wild and free as we sat there all bruised and broken at our own hands. As the gazelles bounded and frolicked, we heard the narrator ask, "But why are they jumping over nothing?" Constance's eyes met mine, and we literally fell over each other in hysterics. I think I remember this so vividly because what made the whole thing absurd had entirely to do with our wretched hangovers juxtaposed with the purity of a nature program. It's a fond memory, but with a bite.

A relative of Constance's, a once-raging lush, didn't drink anymore. This was amazing to me given the fact that I was incapable of going a day without drinking. It could be done, but how? One day I asked. Constance told me her relative went to AA. AA is Alcoholics *Anonymous.* By the dictates of the Eleventh Tradition, I am not supposed to tell you that I got sober in AA. I am supposed to set an example of sobriety and let those in need seek me out, at which point I can direct them to the Twelve Steps. By breaking my anonymity here, I let myself become a representative of the program, which could damage the chances of an alcoholic in need from trying AA simply because he or she doesn't like me personally. Or let's say someone does like me and reads this and decides to try out AA, and then I go out tomorrow and get drunk. What is that person supposed to think then? But statistics for those who stay sober after entering rehab are very poor, about

18 percent. So I am gambling on the notion that my twenty-seven years of sobriety and how it came about might do more good than harm. I'm not promoting AA. I won't wax rhapsodic on its methods or philosophies. It is simply the way I got sober. I really don't care how other people get clean, as long as they're willing to believe that it's possible.

Sick of being hungover, Constance and I attended an AA meeting in my neighborhood sometime in the summer of 1982. It was kind of like the Split Rail—every possible type of character was in there: Bowery bums, guys in suits, East Village bohemians, drag queens. A middle-aged woman went to the front of the room and for half an hour told her story. I cried through the whole thing. And then I went out and got rip-roaring drunk. I cried because that woman had told my story, and I got drunk because I didn't know what else to do. But the seed was planted. I sat in a room full of people who didn't have to drink anymore. I attended meetings off and on for a few months with the notion that I could manage my drinking. I would sit in those meetings, not bothering to get to know anyone, feeling rather smug since maybe I'd gone a night or two without getting drunk. I could control this thing, I figured. I wasn't *that* bad.

Then the following winter, early in 1983, there was a blizzard. I had a stupid fight with a guy I'd been dating and stomped off through the snow that night in a huff. I decided to see the movie *Frances*. You know—Jessica Lange plays Frances Farmer, surely a depressive alcoholic woman with fire and smarts, who ends up having a lobotomy. I guessed I was all right compared to Frances, and after the movie, at the Cottonwood Café, I drank exactly four beers, hardly enough at this point to even get a buzz, but I woke up the next morning completely desperate: suicidal, scared to death, and out of excuses. I said to Constance, "There's a meeting tonight on Perry Street." She said, "Yes, and you are going to it." It wasn't my worst hangover—it hadn't been my worst drunk—but I was finally at the end of my rope. I sat paralyzed for the rest of the day just waiting to go to the meeting. The one time I attempted to go out that day, I slipped on some ice and fell on my ass. It seemed fitting. I had hit bottom, literally.

I went alone to Perry Street that night—Constance didn't get sober for another year. I approached the speaker at the end and could only tell her, "I'm scared." She said to me, "Keep coming back," and that's what I did. I clung to those words. Keep coming back. It seemed so simple. I kept going back, every day to lots of different meetings, and I began to have one sober day after another.

One night I went out with Constance for Mexican food and didn't understand how the hell I could eat it without a beer. I had a miraculous thought: *Today I can try it. Tomorrow may be another story, but today I'll try it.* So I had my first Mexican meal without beer, and I survived.

Once sober, I still did my gigs. I played in bars, but I had some kind of a force field around me. I just was not tempted. All I knew was that my main priority in life was not to drink, because I'd had the revelation that I didn't have a life if I kept drinking. Everything was unmanageable, off track. Up until February 12, 1983, the only thing I'd done with assuredness was drink. I sang because I didn't know what else I could do. I was continually warding off chronic terror. I was unable to have a relationship with a man. I had no real spiritual or moral guidelines. I coped by drinking. It was the constant in my life, the thing that kept me tethered to sanity until it made me insane.

10
Go On and Do It

John Leventhal / Me and John, NYC, 1982

**We both had to see what it means
Whenever two worlds collide.**

With my drinking in remission, by far the most important thing that happened to me after I moved to New York was meeting John Leventhal. Buddy Miller left the band in 1981, so I became the front woman by default and necessity. Without Buddy, though, I was minus a lead guitar player. Our bassist, Lincoln, suggested I give this guy John a call.

John was raised in tony Scarsdale but was now living in the Village. Did I call him? I can't remember, but someone did, and we all met up at Lincoln's Bronx apartment for a rehearsal. Larry Campbell was there, along with our drummer, Karl, and myself and John. We were all still in our twenties, and even then John was a somewhat imposing figure.

He showed up with his Telecaster. He was a beautiful, unique guitar player, and we hit it off musically right away. I know there was one thing in particular that I played that caught his ear—it could have been "The Vigilante" by Judee Sill or "Jesu, Joy of Man's Desiring," which I pitifully tried to tease out of my instrument as though I were Andrés Segovia. John played, and he sounded like Ry Cooder and George Harrison and Hank Williams rolled into one. No matter what we learned that day, when he played, I was moved and transfixed. Every note and chord sent me to the moon. He was fabulous. Whatever we threw his way, he could ace, from country standards to the Beatles. Especially the Beatles. He got the job.

In a way I was already in love. When I think back on the years we spent together as a couple, my strongest feelings about him still have to do with the music. This is the deepest part of what we shared. Something about what we offered each other artistically carried so much more weight than words could communicate. My favorite photograph of John is one I took in Central Park in 1982. He's standing in front of the bandshell, wearing his father's overcoat, next to a portion of some words engraved in the stone surrounding the stage. They say MUSIC LOVER.

I could make John laugh. John's laughter was a joy, an unabashed eruption and fairly easily come by. He loved to laugh, and, try as I might, I could never compete with the guy humor he shared with his pals Zev and Rick and Wells and Donald and Marc. If he was tickled, he would have to stop what he was doing and revel in the hilarity. He'd be laughing so hard he'd be unable to breathe for a minute, doubled over and contorted until his fit had passed.

John was loud. He had a lot to say, and he was confident and passionate and determined, and his style was to speak forcefully and with volume. I could hold the phone a fair distance from my ear while talking to him. One of my favorite memories is of when we were making our first studio album, *Steady On,* and Bruce Hornsby asked John to speak more softly. And for a minute he did.

When he would speak to me about his young nephew back then, he would nearly always choke up, practically unable to contain the longing he had for that little boy's happiness and mourning the intimacy that had been lacking in his own childhood and that he so yearned to give his nephew. It was always clear he wanted children, and with his wife, Rosanne Cash, he's been blessed with his own boy, Jake, his biggest dream come true.

When I met him, John was in a band called Mr. B, one that did original material. John wrote the music, and their lead singer wrote the lyrics along with John. I dubbed their style "horn-rimmed pop," since John was tall and nerdy, wore glasses and loved Steely Dan, the coolest geeks around. When I heard Mr. B, I wanted to throw out the singer and take over the band, which is pretty much what happened eventually.

John was responsible for my becoming a songwriter. We needed each other. He had trouble with singing and lyrics, and I had trouble with writing in general. I had come up with a few things while drunk in Berkeley but had quit trying. Co-writing seemed like a good idea. I desperately wanted to write songs. My heroes were songwriters. I just wasn't a natural at it—I'm still not. It made sense to him to let me try my hand at writing some lyrics to one of his pieces. I needed a push, and horn-rimmed pop seemed like just the ticket.

In the very early days, we did some work at John's old place on West Fourth Street, but it was later, in John's own basement apartment on East Twelfth Street between Second and Third avenues that we started nearly every song we've written together. The apartment was dark and ugly, but it had some square footage, and this was important to John; he needed some space for all his instruments and recording equipment. Not only did John write, but he was an exceptional producer, even back then. Before drum machines existed, John could make a simple track swing with finger snaps and reverb, as was the case with a song called "Nothin' on Me," one of our first efforts and maybe the only early one that survived. It ended up on a record we made called *A Few Small Repairs*.

The apartment had a couch and a chair that John had picked up from home, and we'd sit there, him with a guitar and me with my black-and-white-spotted-cover composition notebooks that I still use to this day. He was a generous, patient, encouraging co-writer, mostly because, I think, there was nothing he would rather have been doing. Most of the time I'd prefer eating glass to trying to write, but for John it was soul sustenance.

The first song John and I wrote was called "The Things She Says," lyrics courtesy of me.

> *It shot like an arrow going straight to my heart,*
> *I'd waited so long for that music to start . . .*

Argh! It was miserable! On my part anyway. Mr. B did the song, and I had become a songwriter, of sorts. We continued, penning such classics as "Strange Feeling," "Lucky Girl," and "There's No Love Like Our Love."

Naturally, with such brilliance afoot, John and I fell in love. We'd been doing both pop and country-band gigs together and had become friends. I was really attracted to him—tall and lanky, loud and cocksure, and handsome, with dark curly hair and green eyes. Of course, when he played that guitar, the heat quotient soared. He asked me out fairly soon after meeting me, but I turned him down because I was hung up on another musician, a doe-eyed songwriter who, as it turned out, was quite the ladies' man. This guy visited me in New York and said he'd write me from across the pond—he was going on tour in Europe—but the letters were not exactly pouring in. John tried to cut to the chase one night after a bunch of us had stayed out until dawn. It was wicked hot outside, and John had air-conditioning in his apartment, an unheard-of luxury, so he offered me a place to sleep.

I had to admit there had been instances of blatant flirtation by John that had made my heart skip a beat, like the time at a Chinese restaurant where he flatly fixed his gaze on me, reached out with his hand, scooped up some of my chow mein, and wordlessly stuffed his face with it. At the movies once, he took a piece of popcorn and stuck it up his nose, again turning to me with the driest, most sober look. Not to be outdone this time, I stuck a piece of popcorn in *my* nose, at which point he swiftly leaned over, plucked it out with his mouth, and ate it. Touché. Clearly there were sparks between us; anyone could see that. But the Roving Dreamboat was due back from Europe the very day John offered me a bed. I had to hold out for Mr. Doe Eyes.

Well, the Casanova Shakespeare arrived at my apartment basically to crash. It didn't feel like much of a reunion, and I began to sense I'd been had, so as he slept, I went through his bag, where I found lots of letters to and from lots and lots of women. I called John and told him. He said, "Well, you were a fool." Hanging my head in shame, I presented myself to John on a platter, and we hooked up. It was the summer of 1982. I was twenty-six years old.

Me and John, 1982

Poor John. He fell for me at a time when I just did not know myself. I was still drinking and had no concept of being the slightest bit of an adult in a relationship. I was surviving. John had focus and confidence, enough to carry me along for a while before all my insecurity started to wear us down, but that was pretty much immediately. He took me to the movie *Brazil* the first week we were together, and I found it so disorienting that I cried through it. Much worse than that, though, was that I blamed him for it! It reminds me of something I think Roger Vadim said about being married to Brigitte Bardot—that she got mad at him in the morning for being rude to her in her dreams the night before. Perhaps I could've pulled this off had I been Brigitte Bardot. John was smart and funny and brilliantly creative, and he loved me and didn't know what to do with me. Almost everything we did together was fraught with some angst from me, from the way he said good-bye on the phone to the way he held my hand to the simple fact that maybe the sky was gray one day. Things were never right; I was not right. Fairly early on in our relationship, I quit drinking, so I was on the proper path, but I had so far to go. We were together off and on for about six years and eventually fizzled out.

Regardless of whatever personal drama was unfolding between us in those days, one thing John and I could always count on was sparking each other creatively, and certainly this is part of how and why we stayed together. We got together regularly and worked on songs. I loved the music John wrote. I would hear words and melodies immediately. It was his confidence and talent and passion that kept me going. I could be furious at him for being insensitive and arrogant, and he would sit down and play "God Only Knows" and I was a goner. I should've seen the writing on the wall when he moved to East Twelfth Street and wouldn't let me have anything to do with picking out his sheets. I broke up with him, and he broke up with me, and so it went until finally, at his behest, it stuck. But months after that, after making our first record and after I moved to the West Village, he came over to my new place for the first time, looked around, and began to cry. I knew why. "I grew up, didn't I?" I said. We knew that our time had passed.

We worked literally for years on the type of pop music I mentioned before, but I knew something was missing. I was still doing gigs in folk rooms and rock clubs and country dives, and if I listed every musical genre I dabbled in for the next couple of years, we'd be here all day. Suffice it to say that the notion of becoming a rockabilly chick with a ponytail and poodle skirts thankfully blew over.

Me and Maria Muldaur as Dinettes,
Pump Boys and Dinettes, *Detroit, 1982*

I even made a quick sojourn to Chapel Hill, North Carolina, in 1996 and joined a band called the Red Clay Ramblers. I first became aware of them in 1985 when I saw *A Lie of the Mind*, a play by Sam Shepard, in New York. The Ramblers performed live during the play—it wasn't a musical; this was a live sound track—

and it was stunning. There was Jack Herrick, Tommy Thompson, Clay Buckner, Bland Simpson, and me. I loved being in the Ramblers. They could do anything. Our sets consisted of all manner of styles, from original stuff to Irish jigs to bluegrass to old gospel songs, complete with five singing parts. We frequented the Carolinas and played the folk festivals along the eastern seaboard and in Canada. We all starred in a musical in Cleveland called *Diamond Studs,* based on the life of Jesse James, in which I played Zee James, Jesse's wife. Jim Lauderdale, a singer-songwriter I'd met in New York, was Jesse, and the Ramblers were his band of outlaws. (Yes, I was trying musical theater, too.) Being in the Ramblers was terrific, but it still wasn't what I was after.

The Red Clay Ramblers, 1986

Diamond Studs, with the Red Clay Ramblers, 1986

So there came a point in my sobriety where I just threw up my hands. I was tired of trying to figure it all out, and thanks to the sober friends I'd made, I didn't see my identity solely as a musician anymore. You go through changes when you quit using, when you quit engaging in the insanity of addiction. Eventually everything kind of comes into question. I mean, you're making this huge choice every day not to do this thing that you were addicted to doing, and that's a powerful experience. I was able to ask myself, *Well, what else am I able to make choices about?* I was stalling with music—I didn't really have any other skills and didn't know how else to make a living, but I wasn't happy showing up to my gigs and playing anymore. I hadn't come to any great revelation about who I was as an artist; I was still a very good copycat and not much else. It seemed pointless and empty to me, and I realized, for the first time in my life, that this doesn't have to be it. I didn't *have* to sing.

The friend who helped me the most was a beautiful, raven-haired, ivory-skinned, blue-blooded New Englander by the name of Kim. Kim was sober, too, had been for three years, which seemed like an eternity to me. I was extremely impressed; I wanted what she had. Kim was probably the first person, besides Stokes, who I let in after I quit drinking. Once I'd stopped, all sorts of problems cropped up, mostly to do with my phobias and panic. Much harder to manage without alcohol. When that stuff hit, I was terrified to be alone and was driven to confide in someone. In fact, I remember the very night that I decided to call Kim and talk to her. I was desperate. And I realized she knew something about me that no one else did—she understood the nature of my anxieties and how they tortured me and ruled my life, because she had the same problems. She called them her "voices." That was such a comfort, that someone else actually had a name for what I was trying to explain. The fact that Kim called our fears "voices" makes us sound a bit schizo, but that wasn't the nature of them. The nature of phobia and panic disorder is to intrude constantly and especially during times of pleasure, like the proverbial devil on the shoulder, but instead of enticing us to behave badly our devils told us we couldn't have fun or be happy, that something could or would go horribly wrong if we tried. These demons lived in our heads every minute; they were our dirty secrets. With Kim not only did I unburden myself of this dark shameful secret, I reveled in knowing I was not alone, which in my opinion is the most healing thing of all. I was not alone. Maybe I wasn't crazy. Kim presented me with this possibility, and it changed my life.

I got a job through Teddy Wainwright, Loudon's sister, as an administrative assistant in a real-estate developer's office and lived the life of a nine-to-fiver. I cut myself loose from all expectations. I still wrote with John and still did one solo gig a week at the Cottonwood Café, but that was all. I felt like I was family in that place. I was comfortable there. I think I got paid forty dollars a night. Oddly, it was the location of my last drink. So it doesn't make a lot of sense, but it was a homey place for me to go.

That decision brought about a turning point eventually. I had been taking stock in this year that I took off. What am I good at? What do I like? How do I want to spend my life? What do I want? I was at an AA meeting at the Church of the Ascension, an Episcopal church on Fifth Avenue and Tenth Street, when I heard a song that I recognized and liked, and I had the distinct revelation that I missed performing. I didn't want to go back to the potpourri, scattershot career I had, but I also knew that I didn't want to move on in my life without having ever tried to find out what kind of artist I really was.

It came to me pretty quickly. I was a solo performer, and part of the epiphany was that I was good by myself; it was the truest form of my talent. That was clear to me, but it was a challenge, because what I was gearing myself up to do was write, and write confessionally, because that's what I loved and had cut my teeth on. It was time to get personal. I could feel it. I knew what the direction had to be.

I had grown up on solo singer-songwriters who played acoustic guitars. I could entertain a roomful of people by myself, and my guitar playing was unique. I was comfortable this way, much more comfortable than fronting a band no matter how much I loved pop and rock and soul. It was that pesky songwriter part that still had me tripped up. But wait. There was one thing. A song I wrote in my head when I'd first moved to New York. I'd written it on the D train to the Bronx one day on my way to a Buddy Miller rehearsal at Lincoln's. I'd been lonely and bereft, and I'd imagined myself singing to a baby—of course the baby was me. I wrote four verses, chords, and a melody, all in my head, and never much thought about it afterward. Because I was not a writer, not then. Now, though, I considered playing it. It was called "I Don't Know Why."

The next challenge was taking this new identity and making it work with John. I don't believe he was aware of what I was trying to do—at any rate, he gave me a new piece of music, fully produced, that had a rhythm-and-blues feel to it, kind of like "Gimme Some Lovin'." It had a simple bluesy chord progression, and I had the idea of trying to morph it into a Richard Thompson song by lowering the E strings down to D to make it drone. Richard had become my reason for living. I changed the beat and turned it into a march instead of a swagger. So I had successfully transposed a Leventhal production piece into a solo acoustic piece, a first. Now lyrics.

The first words that came out of my mouth were, "As a little girl, I came down to the water with a little stone in my hand. . . ." Oh, God! What is THAT? A little girl and a little stone, how twee! Donald Fagen would never sing that line. I called John immediately and played it for him, expecting the worst. He said, "You've got something, keep going." That was a crucial moment, because if he'd said he didn't get it, I probably wouldn't have finished the song.

I realized I was writing about getting sober, about coming alive, about claiming myself and uncovering these gifts that had been obscured by both external and internal forces, about this veil of confusion and dysfunction and addiction being peeled away, bit by bit. Before that I didn't have a message. The song was "Diamond in the Rough," and Shawn Colvin, the singer-songwriter, had found her voice. It was a very pointed incident, this transformation into becoming a songwriter. There was a lot of water under the bridge leading up to it, but it was certainly a very specific point in time, an epiphany for sure, when a line was crossed, and I got it.

I got it!

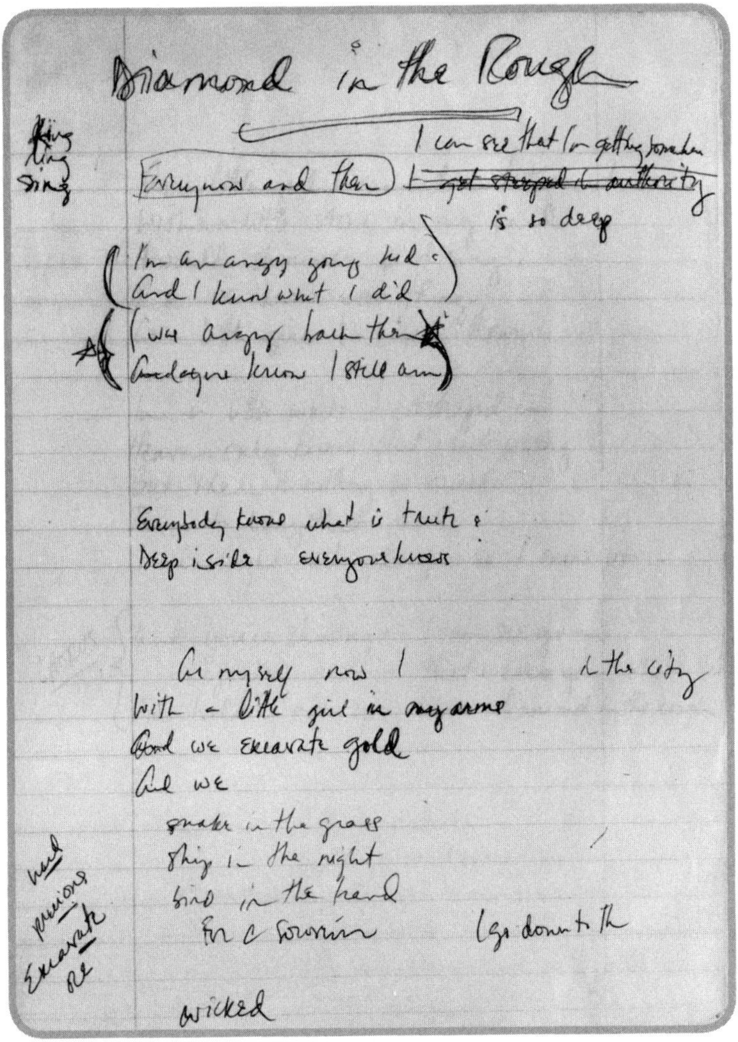

Lyrics from my notebook for "Diamond in the Rough"

11
A Mission

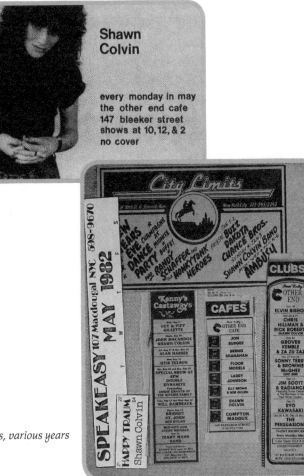

Various gigs, various years

Truth to tell and time to burn, I hit the wall at every turn.
The ceiling cracked in half and I just flew.
Poetry was what I heard, I was hanging on to every word.
I was a lover for the world to woo.

I had a formula for writing songs, and it was nothing profound. It
was so simple, even though the actual writing often is not. It really
came down to trust. I remember writing affirmations back then: *"I,
Shawn Colvin, know everything I need to know to write. I, Shawn
Colvin, am a songwriter. I, Shawn Colvin, have something worth-
while to say."* We were all into affirmations at the time. My friend
Kate Markowitz, who sings with James Taylor, was instructed by
her therapist to make a list of ten things she liked about herself.
Kate went to Starbucks, stared at the paper, wrote down three
things, began to daydream, got a latte, and left without remember-
ing to take the list with her. I dated a guy for a minute, an actor,
who called me one afternoon and said, "I was late to rehearsal! I
was doing affirmations in the mirror, and I started to like myself so
much I lost track of time!" He wanted to be a songwriter, too, and
had given me a tape of something he'd written that I thought was
not good. I called Stokes and asked, "What am I going to do?" He
suggested that I simply pick out the parts that were okay and say
something about those bits, ignore the rest. When I told Stokes that
this fellow had rhymed "apocalypse" with "Picasso lips," there
was a brief pause. Then: "What are you going to do?"

Once I'd written "Diamond in the Rough," I had parameters:
Don't think, sing. Be personal, tell the truth. Remember that
guitar parts are as important as the words and melody. The next
song John gave me didn't need any tweaking or transposing. It
was a minor-key, finger-picked folk song with a wonderful melody
already written by John. Again I tuned the low E string down to

D, so when the verses and choruses hit the major fifth, a D chord, the bass would ring out. I needed a way in lyrically. I'd wanted to use the word "avalanche" in a song, I thought it was a good word. Again, like with "Diamond," I kind of cleared my head, played the guitar, and let something come out of my mouth. This time it was "I'm riding shotgun down the avalanche." It felt good, and the meaning seemed pretty obvious to me: My romance with John was going *down*. It was a song of heartbreak, that much was clear. If I were falling down an avalanche, then there would have to be mountains and snow and a great area of empty space, a void. But the singer is a passenger, and the person at the wheel has sealed her fate, left her nowhere else to go but into the abyss. So I had something close to my heart, I had an interesting metaphor to anchor me, and I had a visual. From there I tinkered with it and filled in the blanks. It might seem strange to have co-written a song with someone about breaking up with that someone, but for some reason it didn't bother me. It was cathartic, and anyway, John knew how I felt. The intent of the song wasn't reconciliation; it was simply a statement, one that felt right.

I'm of the belief that a song isn't really a song until you've tried it out on an audience, any kind of audience, not so much because you want approval—although that's definitely a plus—but because, for me at least, the act of performing a new song in front of people is the ultimate bullshit detector. If there's a lyric I'm uneasy about, I can sense pretty quickly if it's something that's going to work. Or not. I don't mind being uncomfortable, but lines that are just filler or, worse, dishonest, have to be dealt with harshly. Now I was writing, but who was listening?

Along with redefining myself artistically, I had to rethink my venues. It'd been fine to cut my teeth for years at the Other End and Kenny's Castaways on Bleecker Street and the Cottonwood Café on Bank Street, where I could make a few bucks, get some dinner, and see friends. They were all great hangs. There might be an audience present, and there might not be—if I did have a crowd, they might listen, but they might not. I used the times when they weren't there or weren't paying attention to mess around with strange covers or even little pieces of songs I tried to write, and this phase of my career shaped me as much as anything, but it was time to move on.

There was another place called the Speakeasy over on MacDougal. It was still a joint, but with a higher calling—the Speakeasy wanted to hire songwriters, and its patrons, for the most part, wanted to hear them. In fact, the club was spawned by a group called the Songwriters Exchange that met weekly at an apartment belonging to Jack Hardy. I wasn't part of the group, but I knew of some of its members: David Massengill, Cliff Eberhardt, Richard Meyer, Christine Lavin, Rod MacDonald, John Gorka, Tom Intondi, Frank Christian, and, probably most notably, Suzanne Vega. I'd also met Lucy Kaplansky, who, like me, didn't write much at that time but was keen to interpret the songs of some of those other writers and did so without peer. We were individual performers, but some of my fondest memories are singing "Ring of Fire" or "The Return of the Grievous Angel" with Lucy at the Cottonwood, or of huddling with her and John Gorka in a back room at the Speakeasy, working on harmony parts to his songs.

This community of writers also put together an organization called Fast Folk, a monthly "musical magazine," which was actually a vinyl recording, showcasing the fruits of their labors. In addition, somebody somewhere, I don't know who, had the idea of putting on a Fast Folk concert, a revue consisting of several different performers who'd been featured on the albums. Remember that song, the one I wrote in my head on the subway? Fast Folk chose that song, "I Don't Know Why," to be recorded for their magazine and invited me to sing it at their concert. This was huge,

I can't tell you how much so, as the show was to be at the famous Bottom Line, a true listening room, a concert venue. And I was getting to sing a song I wrote. The show also played in Boston, and the visit there turned out to be enormously important for me. At the after-show party, I was introduced to Bob Donlin.

Bob Donlin was a crotchety marshmallow of an ex–Beat poet, who, along with his wife, Rae Ann, devoted himself to a tiny coffeehouse near Harvard Square in Cambridge called Passim, where listening was serious business. There was no liquor there—you were coming in to have some cider and cake and to listen to a troubadour, a folksinger, a singer-songwriter, whatever you want to call it. Its audiences were more than respectful; they were by turns reverential and adoring. They wanted to hear original music. Bob had been impressed enough with my performance at the Fast Folk show to offer me a weekend as an opening act for Greg Brown, a hunky and marvelous baritone from Iowa who wrote great songs. I was to play Friday night, Saturday night, Sunday afternoon, which was a live radio broadcast, and Sunday night. He offered me three hundred fifty dollars, and I was over the moon.

I had exactly three original songs—"I Don't Know Why," "Shotgun Down the Avalanche," and "Diamond in the Rough"— not enough, but I'd have to figure something out. I figured something out. I pulled out every obscure cover song I could think of that I'd done in the bars. I've been a huge John Hiatt fan since discovering Ry Cooder's version of "The Way We Make a Broken Heart," and I played "It Hasn't Happened Yet" and "Your Crazy Eyes" by Hiatt. I played "American Jerusalem" by Rod MacDonald and a song or two written by my old boyfriend Jim. I'd been doing an acoustic version of the old Foundations hit, "Baby, Now That I Found You," forever. Down the line Alison Krauss would hear me do it at the Telluride Bluegrass Festival and record my arrangement. There were songs that I later recorded on an album of covers, like "You're Gonna Make Me Lonesome When You

Go" by Dylan, "Satin Sheets" by Willis Alan Ramsey, "There's a Rugged Road" and "The Vigilante" by the brilliant Judee Sill, and one of my favorites from the Buddy Miller Band days, "Killin' the Blues" by Roly Salley, also covered by Alison and Robert Plant as well as John Prine and who knows who else. It's a perfect tune without a single rhyme in it, and it doesn't make a bit of difference. That's poetic songwriting. There was one Colvin/Leventhal song called "Knowing What I Know Now"—kind of a mouthful anyway—and I'd do that one. I ended with "Diamond in the Rough." They bought it. No one called the songwriter police.

I had no idea how to talk to an audience when I started playing Passim. So I did the same thing I did when I started playing the guitar. I went to school, this time by watching performers like Greg Brown and Claudia Schmidt in listening situations, trying to pick up tricks and clues and methods of how to build a relationship with the audience. I can't overstate the impression Greg Brown left on me after that first weekend at Passim in the spring of 1987. I watched every one of his shows as if they were master classes. Greg knew who he was onstage—that was the main thing—and he knew his audience. There's an art to handling your crowd, especially when it's only you and you can hear a pin drop. I was quaking. Greg had his stories, his one-liners; he had his timing and dynamics down. He was accessible. Instinctively, I knew that's what I had to go for. Some artists can reel you in by being remote, but I'm like a dog—I just want you to like me.

When you're out there onstage all by yourself, the audience is all you've got. If you want them to truly get what you're doing up there, you need to know how to reach out to them. Nowadays it can be hard sometimes to shut me up onstage, and I like to say that the saving grace is that I've been in therapy so long that I just naturally wind down forty-five minutes into the set. Back then, though, I had to plan what to say. The whole thing was nerve-racking and thrilling.

Now, here's the bottom line: Donlin wanted me back in about eight weeks' time. And if there's one thing I was sure of, it was that I *had* to have at least one new original song by then; my pride depended on it. I felt like I owed it to the Passim audience to grow, to have a larger catalog, to become a surer and more authentic songwriter. Of course I wanted that anyway, but, ever the procrastinator, I needed a deadline, and whenever my next gig at Passim was, that was my deadline. Pretty soon I had five songs, then seven. Bob Donlin and the audiences at Passim were invaluable to me because of that. Their expectations were higher than mine.

Bob and Rae Ann Donlin at Passim, Cambridge, MA, 1987

I started developing a fan base there, until I got a headlining gig and people were opening for me. All of this was before I made a record. Pretty soon I'd be playing theaters in Cambridge, not coffeehouses, and the first time I did was in September 1988, at Paine Hall on the Harvard campus, capacity 435. I put a white carnation on every seat.

Another reason the Boston area was such fertile ground for someone like me was the presence of college radio, like stations WERS from Emerson College and WUMB from UMass Boston. I had a little cassette demo with four songs on it, and these guys played it, along with the Fast Folk recording of "I Don't Know Why." (Incidentally, Alison Krauss and Union Station did a cool bluegrass version of that song in 1992 on their album *Every Time You Say Goodbye*.) Those radio stations were the best marketing tool I could have had and helped immeasurably in building a following for me.

Philadelphia Folk Festival, 1988

Then I got a call in October 1987. Suzanne Vega had hit it big with "Luka," and we were all atwitter. I'd actually sung on the record. I remember going into a coffee shop and hearing "Luka" playing on the radio, I could hear my little "ah" part. It lit fires under all of us; it was inspiring. It also made us jealous, which is never a bad thing. I remember going to see Jane Siberry in concert at the Bottom Line during that same period of time and walking out devastated, because I just felt like I couldn't begin to be that cool—but those are good things, they make you try. I got a call from Suzanne's manager saying that she was on tour, didn't have a backup singer, and that she'd kind of like to add one. The next leg of her tour was to be all over Europe for November and December. Now, I was bound and determined not to commit to another job that would take me away from the matter at hand, which was finally doing my very own thing. But Good Lord. I'd been to Canada. That was the extent of my foreign travel. Two months in Europe, on a proper tour? I couldn't pass it up.

I met the king of Sweden and members of Twisted Sister. I saw more cathedrals and museums than you can shake a stick at. I went running along the Seine and the Rhine, in the Alps, past Buckingham Palace, by Irish potato fields. I saw where each Beatle lived. I had an affair with a drummer who was a terrible scoundrel. We saw movies in Rome, made love to "Tunnel of Love" in Antwerp, fought in Brighton. I bought red gloves in Germany, black jeans in Switzerland, chocolate in Belgium. I listened to *Nothing Like the Sun* by Sting and *A Walk Across the Rooftops* by the Blue Nile. And I got to sing in some of the most beautiful old theaters you ever saw.

Suzanne Vega, 1987

If I had been hungry to become "someone" before Suzanne's tour, I was starving now. I came home to New York two months later a little bruised from the road and the affair, but eons richer. Thank you, Suzanne. I felt even more under the gun to buckle down and get serious. Certainly that drive was aided by seeing what Suzanne had done. As my sister, Kay, would say, it gave me the *wantin'*. She says you've got to have the wantin', but she also says you can't have it too bad or it can ruin things. So I tried to stay focused and wrote another song with John, called "Steady On."

12
She's All Right

CBS says YES, 1988—John Leventhal, me, and Steve Addabbo

Gee, it's good to see a dream come true.

It must've been about June 1988. The Polaroid is of John and me and one of my managers, Steve Addabbo. We're outside John's studio on Twelfth Street, holding a bottle of sparkling cider. I wrote a caption on it, and it reads *"C*B*S says Y*E*S."*

As it turned out, the Suzanne Vega tour yielded a far bigger dividend than just goosing me to get on the horn with my own career. Her managers, Ron Fierstein and Steve Addabbo, took an interest in me and casually gave my four-song demo tape to Joe McEwen at Columbia Records. Joe was an A&R guy there, which meant he could sign acts, and he loved the tape. Columbia signed me, and Ron and Steve wanted to manage me. It all happened really fast.

Shawn Colvin

1. Diamond in the Rough
2. I Don't Know Why
3. Another Long One
4. Shotgun Down the Avalanche
5. American Jeruselum

SHAWN COLVIN

1. © Colvin/Leventhal
2. © Colvin
3. © Colvin
4. © Colvin/Leventhal
5. © R. MacDonald

212-254-4354
91 E. 3RD ST. # 24
NY NY 10003

The demo tape that got me signed

One of the first things I did was . . . move. At long last I left my rat- and roach-infested East Village apartment that had been home for eight years and relocated across town to a considerably nicer place in the West Village. I cried my eyes out while waiting in that empty Third Street hellhole for the cable man to come and shut down the service. I thanked that wretched place for allowing me to do the hardest growing up of my life. I'd been drunk and suicidal. I'd been sober and suicidal. I'd been through the deepest and most difficult relationship of my life, with John. I'd started therapy with Myra Friedman, whom I still talk to. I'd written the first significant song of my life, "Diamond in the Rough," which defined everything I would write from then on. I forged friendships that would last forever. I'd had countless odd jobs and eventually landed a recording contract. I learned to be myself. So why could I not see that I would simply be bringing that self to increased square footage, a bathtub in an actual bathroom, an actual living room with a view, and no rodents? But there you have it.

Anyway, I had more important things to worry about. At thirty-two years old (Columbia suggested I list my age as thirty, and I did), I was finally going into the studio to make my own record, and even though I'd been in studios before to sing on other people's records or demos, this just seemed ultimately like the real deal. The stakes couldn't get any higher.

We decided to record "Diamond in the Rough" and "Shotgun Down the Avalanche" first, since, being the oldest songs, they had received the most thought and preproduction. After I'd nailed down the acoustic guitar tracks for both of them, the day came when it was time to do the vocals, and I was pretty apprehensive. We dimmed the studio lights and lit candles in the vocal booth. I probably said a prayer, or at least an affirmation: "I, Shawn Colvin, have all I need inside me not to fuck up this vocal. . . ." We were doing "Avalanche" first. I put on headphones while John and the engineer picked a microphone for me and gave me a mix I felt good singing to. The rubber was about to meet the road. I closed my eyes and took a deep breath and laid down my first vocal take on "Shotgun" for the album we would call *Steady On*. When the song ended, I opened my eyes and waited for the verdict from the control room. I should mention that normally you sit down to do vocals and perform several attempts, then go through each take, making notes about which lines are sung best in each pass. From there you "comp" the vocal—pick out the best bits and marry them into one complete take. But I was too nervous to do a bunch of passes; I needed to know how that first one was. Was I in good form or was I self-conscious? When I walked into the control room to listen, I saw very long faces and was crestfallen. I was sure this meant I'd sucked—but no. Turns out the engineer did not press the Record button. There was nothing to listen to. I can laugh about it now, but we had to end the session for the day, and I never saw the engineer again—that's how far it threw me. I guess somebody got rid of him. I've learned since to see the wisdom in not overthinking a performance, that sometimes vocally what may seem like a mistake can actually hold some emotional value, but back then I was beyond nitpicky. I would sometimes comp the vocal, not line by line, not even word by word, but syllable by *syllable*. Today I would rather chew tinfoil than go to that trouble. If you really can sing, there isn't the need for that kind of microscopic attention, but back then, forget it. I was a total control freak about the singing.

John and I were no longer a couple. As musical partners this was our shot, but our breakup was complete by the time we were finishing *Steady On*. As you can imagine, that made for some tense studio sessions. Part of me viewed John as the enemy, because he was so bloody sure of himself and I didn't have the maturity to experience that as anything but a power play. John knew it was "my" record, that I had to be happy, but he was also hired to be the overseer of the thing, and rightly so. These days, when we record or write together, if I think he's acting arrogant I just threaten to slap him, but back then I threw pizza in his general direction or cried. And John? You know how men can compartmentalize and still tend to the job at hand in the midst of Armageddon? It drove me crazy.

In the end, we did at least some of the work in separate studios. I banished him from the vocal sessions, which I slugged out with an engineer for weeks and weeks. I produced one track on my own, "Another Long One," and asked my friend Bob Riley to produce "Stranded," both of which I'd written by myself.

One of the things I'd loved about all the records I grew up listening to was looking at the back cover credits for the guests who appeared on them, like when Joni Mitchell and James Taylor hooked up and sang for each other on "Blue" and "Mud Slide Slim," respectively. In addition to the fine rhythm section we had, with the late T-Bone Wolk on bass and Jerry Marotta on drums, I got Suzanne and Lucy Kaplansky to sing on "Diamond in the Rough." Soozie Tyrell played violin and sang on "Another Long One," and Bruce Hornsby stopped by one day to play piano. Earlier that year Bruce had performed at a Grateful Dead tribute concert (oh, joy) at Madison Square Garden, one that Suzanne was performing at as well, so my managers, Ron and Steve, got me backstage. I was after Hornsby in particular, because I loved his record *The Way It Is,* and there he was. I handed him that same lucky, ratty tape that had gotten me signed to Columbia. I figured it was a long shot, but two days later I got a phone call from none other than Hornsby, telling me how much he liked the tape. He agreed to come in and play on "Something to Believe In," and Leventhal and I behaved, for that day anyway.

It took nearly a year to make *Steady On.* We started the album in the fall of 1988 and finished the following spring, with Kevin Killen doing the mixes. Besides "Diamond" and "Shotgun," these are the songs we recorded, along with how some of them came to be in the first place:

John gave me the music that was to be the title song. "Steady on" is an English phrase that means to steady oneself, and I heard it first as the title of a dance program I had a small part in by a New York troupe called XXY. John's music seemed bouncy and purposeful, and I just knew that "Steady On" would fit as the chorus refrain.

I brought the song with me on a little beach trip to a friend's house in North Carolina and got the first lines sitting by the ocean. I took it from there and just juxtaposed imagery of weaving and wandering that hopefully got pulled taut and straight at the chorus. At the time, I didn't write many "fun" songs, but this one was light and had a smile. Even the doomed love affair in the second verse is left in the dust by the chorus. John's production is superb here, from all the intricate percussive touches to the modal tribal yells he sings in the chorus. This song was debuted at the Newport Folk Festival in 1989.

The song "Stranded" started with the guitar part that opens it, which reminded me a little bit of "Waiting on a Friend" by the Rolling Stones. Often, if you can get one good line or verse right at the beginning, the song will be set up well for you. In this case, outer space came into play on the second line, so I had my little metaphor that gave me security. The song is another vehicle for my failing relationship with John, and I appreciate the tenderness and blameless quality about it. I wrote this one alone.

Another solo effort, and one I really feel I've underestimated over the years, is "Another Long One," inspired by either John or the Doe-Eyed Dreamboat—I can't remember which. This was an old song, something I started to write before "Diamond in the Rough" but didn't finish until I got my songwriting legs under me. The first line makes no grammatical sense—"If losing sleep were any indication of the loving that I've missed . . ." I supposed it should be "If loss of sleep," which sounds like it's got a pole up its rear end. I let stuff like that slip by whenever possible if it's something that just flies out. Better to leave it. There's a line like that in "Shotgun": "This is the best thing and the very most hard." Huh? But it felt right; it came out of my mouth correctly. "Another Long One" speaks to that basic hard truth about yourself when all is said and done. My boyfriends weren't perfect, but it was becoming clear to me that I had some pretty significant issues in the intimacy department. I was massively insecure for one thing, prone to self-righteousness, victimization, and obsession—hence the "little boys in my head sleeping tight"—tending to look on the dark side of possibility when I didn't understand men (which was often), ultimately creating a no-win train of thought: "If I think that you are with me / Then I know that you can always change your mind." This makes for long nights indeed. Just me and my well-intentioned spite. Not so cozy. The girls like this one. John thinks I've outgrown it, but it feels as right today as it did twenty-three years ago. I perform it often. And for the album I produced it myself with the wonderful percussionist Michael Blair, who literally beats on pots and pans here, the clanging of my own warped mind.

I'd say the cornerstone of *Steady On* is "Diamond in the Rough" and this theme of healing and recovery. "Cry Like an Angel" is a chip off that block. John had written it and even had some chorus lyrics: "I hear you callin', you don't have to talk so loud, / I see you fallin', and you don't have to walk so proud, / You can run all night but I can take you where / You can cry like an angel . . ." That was all he had, but it got me. It started with mandolin, and I wanted it to sound like a Band song—I wanted to hear Rick Danko sing it. That's what I reached for lyrically, using colloquialisms like "It's not so's you'd notice" and "There were hard pills to swallow / But we drank 'em all down," bringing in a mystery train and the wheels of ambition, the Friday night, dances, and even a band. The theme is self-discovery and the beginnings of self-reliance and a certain maturity gained as a result of having gone through the fire. So this song was about grief and the necessity of grieving. We can cry like angels when there are no words.

"The Story" is a good song. I'm proud of that song. I'm proud of it because it wasn't easy to write, but I managed a lyrically beautiful portrait—albeit one-sided, I admit—of what was hard at home. The story that was mine to tell is of my experience growing up, and it was certainly fraught. My father was angry, my mother was trapped.

Whereas I tended to blame myself early on for any upheaval, in my teens and twenties the picture began to balance out more, due in no small part to the discovery of my sister's friendship. She gave me some perspective no one else in the family could or would—maybe it wasn't all me. So I wrote the song to her. I've got our father hiding in the basement and our mother being a housewife cooking for us upstairs. I put my mother in a cast-iron dress in an effort to be sympathetic about the role that she and her generation of women were forced to take on in the 1950s: expected to marry early, have children, and become housewives. It was as burdensome for my mother as for the next person, and she really had more potential and better ideas than were allowed her back then.

At the end, I used the color red as a tool for pulling some things together—one of them being courage, one of them being heart, one of them being my sister's skin—she's very Native American–esque. And using red as a metaphor, or as a symbol, for blood, which I say in the end is thicker than water. The family bond remains. After I got sober and entered therapy, it seemed as if all any of us had was our stories, and that we qualify to exist and to take up space and to tell them. This was mine. I was born to be telling this story. I do regret saying, "I seem to be nobody's daughter." I was going through a process of trying to define myself, and it was essential right then that I reject whatever version of "daughter" I'd played up until that time. The sick one, the troubled one, the one you shake your head over. It was time to let it go, and in so doing I lyrically disowned Mom and Dad. I'm sorry for that. Believe me, I've tried to stop loving my family. It doesn't work.

When I was still living in my apartment in Greenwich Village, my father called out of the blue one day and said, "Write whatever you want to write." I think in his own way he was letting me know that he knew it hadn't been easy and that he was willing to accept some responsibility. A few years later, when I was living in Venice, California, he called again. This time he asked what it was like for me growing up. "If you still want to know tomorrow morning, call me back," I said. I was really going to tell him the truth, and I wanted to be sure he wanted to hear it. I wasn't sure if he would actually call, but sure enough my phone rang the following morning, and it was my father on the line. We had a short but healing conversation.

I hope I have outgrown all this at this point. Being a parent—if that doesn't give you some perspective and a little bit of forgiveness, then you're made of stone. It's hard. I don't care what anybody says. There's no manual. I was forty-two when I had my child, so I don't have the excuse of being too young. My mother and I are much closer now than we ever were. I know she's proud of me. My parents moved to Austin when my sister was pregnant with Grace, so they also were there when Callie was born, and then when my niece Frances, Kay's second daughter, came along six months later. They are called Mimi and Papa, which sort of represents a new birth for them, too, becoming grandparents. All of us have new roles now. It's been enlightening to say the least, to have my mother watch me parent and for me to watch her grandparent. I imagine she gets a kick out of the countless ways I am baffled by this absurd responsibility, and I'm soothed to see how Callie, a little piece of me, loves her Mimi and Papa.

I still love playing "Ricochet in Time." How did I know, drunk in Berkeley and working in stained glass, that I'd be traveling for most of my career? I was weary then, and when I'm weary now, like last Friday when I did two shows in a row at the One World Theater in Austin, "Ricochet" speaks for me and shores me up. Even the line about daydreaming in my room . . . well, it was about my attic room in California, but it's totally about my hotel room now. I didn't take too many planes or know too many names back then, but these days I sure do. How did I know? I just sat up in that room drinking beer and out it came, the first two verses, on my Martin D-28. Nearly ten years later, I wrote the last verse in New York on East Third Street. I'm still amazed it survived all that time and that it shows no signs of fading. Transformation and travel. It still gets me.

When I got home from touring Europe with Suzanne in January of 1988, I was beat but I was full, full of longing to be a star, full of the rain in London and the churches in Italy and the dark mornings in Stockholm. Oh, my goodness, I felt worldly. My view out the window on Third Street looked smaller. There was such a vast universe out there—how was I going to be part of it? I knew that the only thing for it was pen to paper. This was now my job. I had jet lag, and I couldn't sleep. I played guitar and lit candles and longed for my life to start, longed for the crazy drummer who escorted me through Europe, longed to go back there. I played some chords and sang, "It is the dead of the night, the dead of the night"—which it was. Then I did something new. I became a character in my own song, someone not me. I became Eleanor Rigby, one of all the lonely people, who sat in her room in London at night alone with her pen and paper. She had a life, too.

John and I had a major tiff about "Dead of the Night."

He had written an interlude for the guitar solo where the song changed keys. It was beautiful, but he wanted to be co-credited as a writer on the song. I was ultraprotective of the stuff I'd written alone, mostly because I could hardly believe I'd even done it, and John's wanting credit just about undid me in the power-struggle department. I reared up and told him he could shove his interlude, and he backed down. The interlude stayed, and I kept sole credit as songwriter. You can imagine how the room looked after that standoff.

For as long as I can remember I've kept composition notebooks, the kind with the black-and-white splattery covers. Not as a kid, but by the time I made my living in bands I was keeping them. I wrote down lyrics to songs I needed to learn, to songs I wanted to learn (think twice before you tuck into "It's All Right, Ma"), set lists, phone numbers, and all the games we'd play between sets, our favorite being a complicated affair we called the Alphabet Name Game.

Then I started writing with John and the composition notebooks took on new meaning. I actually composed—badly, perhaps, but I did. I suppose I have fifteen to twenty of them. With each new record I'd start a new one, so I have all the drafts of the songs I've written and drafts of ones I've never finished, like "Hurricane." Maybe one day I'll finish it. They live in my music room in varying states of decay.

Steady On was released on October 17, 1989, the same day as the earthquake in San Francisco. It was time for "the push." It really amuses me now to remember my naïveté about the actual business of promoting a product—the product being me. I was on a huge label, Columbia, and they had the means to send me hither and yon to promote the record and to get me on TV, which was what they did. My little world was about to get much bigger.

I performed the song "Steady On" on both Letterman and Carson. It takes all day to rehearse for sound and camera blocking. Then you get dressed and made up, and then you wait till nearly the end of the show, when the music is slated to be taped. For three minutes you play your song on national television, and then you are done. It goes by *fast*. After the Carson show was over and I was walking back to my dressing room, Freddy De Cordova, *The Tonight Show*'s producer, walked beside me and thanked me for being on the show. I was still breathless and cooed back, "Oh, thank you for having me!" which must have been the oldest setup line in the book. He growled back, with a lascivious grin, "I've never had you!" Welcome to Old Hollywood.

A few weeks after I was on *Letterman* for the first time, I got a call from his producer; their musical act for the evening had canceled. Could I come in and do a song—like, right now? This is one of my fondest memories. I put on a thrift-shop green-printed minidress, some little black pumps, a Kangol hat because I was having a bad-hair day, slopped on some makeup and went up to the studio, walked onstage, and played "Diamond in the Rough," solo, no rehearsal—not necessary, since it was just me. Playing solo was something I was 100 percent comfortable with. I don't mean to brag, but after I was done, David Letterman announced on the show that he wanted to marry me. He never followed up, though, the big tease. I think it was the minidress. Now it was time to head out on the promotional tour.

First I tackled the USA and learned about the real job of being a salesman. Radio was still a key factor in the success of an artist like me, that and relentless touring in hopes of creating a grass-roots following built on hard work, not hype, of loyal fans, station by station and city by city. We reached out primarily to an album-cut-oriented format called Triple A radio, but Columbia believed I could possibly cross over to other, wider-reaching formats, like Top 40, which produced hits. The record company had radio representatives that covered different areas of the country. I would travel from one major market to another, and even some not-so-major ones, visiting any radio station that would see me, and thanks to Columbia a lot of them would. Once there I'd usually sing a couple songs live on the air and do a short interview. I'd do two or three of these a day. Then there was press, which meant taking up residence in a hotel bar and speaking with any publication that might be willing to talk to me. (I think my personal record was nineteen interviews in a row in Oslo.) At night I would do a show, sometimes in a tiny club where nobody came out to see me. That's how you did it in those days. It was about making literal connections instead of virtual ones. It was a crazy amount of work, but it's what you signed up to do, and thank God for it, because building my career slowly and steadily is at least part of the reason I've had some longevity.

But all the years of climbing into vans and going to crummy little dives and staying in worse motels didn't prepare me for this. Maybe it was the isolation, maybe it was the pressure of finally getting my shot, or the weirdness of selling myself, or the inevitable exhaustion, but I wore down quick. After two months of it, I got a break at Christmas and just cratered. The depression was back, and instead of feeling rejuvenated because of the time-out, I actually sank further down. I remember sitting in the kitchen on West Fourth Street frantically talking on the phone to my friends, perusing self-help books. I was plagued by bleak thoughts, daily crying jags, and the undeniable sense that I did not have another round of promo in me. I might have been able to manage it if I could just have stopped, but now was definitely not the time to stop. This was it. I'd worked all my life for this.

My therapist, Myra, insisted I see someone who could prescribe an antidepressant for me, so I went to some pasty psychiatrist who gave me Prozac. Just like magic, three weeks later I was not only well, I was supercharged. Did most people walk around feeling this sense of overall well-being and optimism? I mean, it was really heaven.

Prozac was a great gift to me. I had many, many productive years writing songs, making and promoting records, traveling the world under its effect. The notion that this kind of drug can take away one's creative spirit is caca to me. I thrived on it.

With the New Year, 1990, came new promise and new goals—I was going global. I went on my first international promotional trip, which I will never forget. The label was having a big conference in Sydney, Australia, and I was one of the new artists picked to go. It was a dream before I even got there—I was flown first class on Qantas. I could write this whole book about flying first class on Qantas. I had never flown first class *anywhere*. I was in a massive seat in the nose of a 747 with lovely Australian flight attendants feeding me and doting on me. I was thirty-two, but I might as well have been five. After being given steak and ice cream and chocolate for dinner, I was tucked in for the night. We flew over the South Pacific, and I woke up to a steaming cup of coffee with a view of the sun rising over Fiji out my window.

We came in to land over the red rooftops of Sydney, and I was shown how real men party. I will only say that there were goats in hotel rooms and that the mantra of the convention was "I'll sleep when I'm dead." I was thoroughly charmed by the Australians and by the country itself—it was February and high summer, and Sydney was a tropical paradise. The convention moved at one point from Sydney to Hamilton Island on the Gold Coast, and I took a helicopter to the Great Barrier Reef to snorkel. Honestly, I still can't believe it. We got dropped off on a plank in the middle of the ocean, where they tossed us some snorkel gear and dumped us overboard. It was spectacular.

From Australia I flew to Stockholm (the worst jet lag of all time; I was practically hallucinating) and all through Europe, doing much the same drill as I had in America, but with more exotic locations and languages. It was grueling, but so utterly enchanting. I was on stages in London and Amsterdam and Milan and Dublin and Glasgow and Oslo and Madrid and Hamburg, doing my show and my songs. By the time I got back to New York, I'd been nominated for a Grammy in the Best Contemporary Folk category.

On February 21, 1990, I took Stokes with me to the Grammy Awards at Radio City Music Hall. I won. I still have the cassette tape from my answering machine that night. I just listened to it. Congratulations from so many! John, Kim, of course. My lawyer and my therapist! Buddy and Julie yelling "Yeehaw!" T-Bone Wolk, folks from back home in Carbondale. I'm struck by the outpouring of joy for me in these messages, and I feel so much pride in this achievement, more now than then, in fact. Just an award, yeah, but it was a proclamation. I turned out all right.

First Grammy night, 1990

At a function the night before the awards show, I ran into Bonnie Raitt backstage—I'd never met her—and she grabbed my arm. "I voted for you," she whispered. The secret's out, Bon! Holy, holy, holy shit. You know what? It just doesn't get any better than that.

13
Days Go By

Larry Klein, 1991

All this time we've been a face in the crowd,
Now we're living in color and laughing out loud.

The First Avenue uptown bus from East Third Street to Thirty-
fourth Street was my mode of transport to visit my therapist,
Myra. I'd been seeing her since 1985, after trying and firing several

numbskulls in the mental-health profession. One, for example, upon hearing me profess to feeling pretty bad, quipped, "What else is new?" Sacked her. No doubt I was boring, but she was getting paid to be bored. I'd also seen an intimidating, butch woman who informed me, as a matter of course, during our first—and last—session that I wasn't allowed to hit her. Oh, okay. Then there was the one who proudly told me I had a "scrappy" personality. She ended sessions by getting up to wash dishes—her office was in her kitchen.

Myra Friedman was smart, funny, perceptive, and grounded, a bubbly Jewish redhead with patience and empathy to spare for all of us neurotic fools. Her place felt safe, I suppose because she felt safe. She has been able all these years to witness and validate my external successes and failures, along with my internal milestones and setbacks, while still managing to confront me gently and steer me carefully toward autonomy and self-awareness.

The time had come for a follow-up record to *Steady On*. I felt then, as I do now, that if *Steady On* were the only record I ever made, I'd be content with that. But clearly another album was expected, which was both thrilling and terrifying. While promoting the first record, I made attempts to remember snippets and bits of lyrics and melodies, some of my own and some from John, so I'd have a slight head start when it came to getting twelve new tracks together. I was on the bus ride to Myra's office, and I was thinking, *God, why can't I just feel the pure, unconditional love of the archetypal mother and be done with this shit?* Then I heard a lyric—"Please no more therapy / Mother take care of me"—and although I didn't have the breakthrough with Myra I was hoping for that day, the line I'd heard in my head and the rhythm to it were locked in. That song became "Polaroids," and it was the last song I would ever debut at Passim. I recall sitting backstage there sometime in 1990, putting the finishing touches on it. I had to have the song ready for my people at Passim so they could see I wasn't a slacker.

The writing process for my sophomore effort had begun, but I didn't know what to do about a producer. Musically the obvious choice was John, but personally I wasn't so sure. We did go into the studio together at one point to begin the next project, but I found I couldn't do it, could not work alongside him or even be in the same room with him. John was over the breakup, but I wasn't. I had to look for another producer.

The only candidate I chose to have a meeting with was Larry Klein, Joni Mitchell's producer, bass player, and husband at the time, which didn't hurt his case. They were making exquisite records, and I had to figure that Joni would suffer no fools—Klein must be sharp. I met with him in New York in late 1990, and he was *quite* sharp, actually.

What I hadn't bargained for was his sense of humor. Klein is a complete and utter goofball who will lean into you and lock eyeballs intensely, then whisper whatever the movie quote of the day is—like "Is it safe?" from *Marathon Man*—followed by gales of laughter. During my tenure with Larry, I was to be inundated with all manner of novelty tapes, from the Jerky Boys' prank calls, to Orson Welles losing it as he does a frozen-peas voice-over, to an extremely blue sexual guide to the signs of the zodiac by Rudy Ray Moore. Larry might, in the middle of a serious discussion, turn to me and say, "Uh, Shawny-Shawn-Shawn, uh, what would you do if, right now, I shat, pissed, came, sneezed, puked, laughed, and cried, all at the same time, what would you do?" He never waited for an answer, being too busy cracking himself up. I managed to throw him once—he was nursing a terrific pimple on his nose, an absolute monstrosity. I looked at him and asked casually, "Are you planning to have a flea circus on that thing?" For a moment he was stumped, until he realized I was referring to the Big Top bulging on the end of his schnozzle. Flustered, and not amused, he said, "Fuck you," and swiveled his chair around to the recording console while the engineer and I rolled on the floor for days.

Larry had a studio, called the Kiva, in his home in Bel Air, and we agreed that this would be the best place to record *Fat City*. Let's just cut to at least part of the chase: Joni Mitchell lived there, too. I was hardly oblivious to that; in fact, I was in a bit of a stupor about it. I wasn't sure I could handle being in such close proximity to my undisputed hero without losing consciousness. I needn't have worried. There's never a lull in the conversation with Joni around. She is an expert storyteller, a master of language, and it was pure joy to listen to her speak in the same poetic yet down-to-earth, streetwise vernacular she used in her songs. She commands your undivided attention, which you're happy to give. Joni is endlessly fascinating, funny, and intense, still like royalty to me, although she will tell you anything. I found out more about her than I could ever have dreamed, about her boyfriends, her career, and her experiences. She's low on bullshit, high on opinions.

I saw her writing a song. Her notebooks were not dissimilar to mine—basic lined paper, notes and lyrics written by hand, but still I could hardly take it in—she was human. I got to see her come into the studio having just woken up, still in her pajamas. We all went out to dinner every night, sometimes to a vegetarian hot spot called À Votre Santé, which Joni referred to as "Mow de Lawn."

When I asked her advice about the fact that my boyfriend had called a live-sex 900 number, she swiftly brought out the I Ching and threw it for me, simultaneously confessing that she once had a perv boyfriend, too. She gave me presents—a photograph from an exhibit she had up at the time and an antique Native American silver necklace of hers. We took a lot of Polaroids and had a technique of peeling the backing off while the photo was still developing so we could mark it up with the side of a nickel. I have a Polaroid of Joni hand-decorated by the lady herself—she embellished her clothed image with breasts and pubic hair.

Joni, 1991

I was fretting over a lyric one day for a song called "Kill the Messenger"—"Sometimes someone drifts by / And our nets get entwined in the . . ." The what? Joni looked at me as though I were heinously dense and shrugged her shoulders. "The sea," she said matter-of-factly. Well, of course. She called me Shawnykins and probably remembers none of this, but I always will. I laughed and ate and talked with Joni Mitchell. Even now I can hardly believe it, but then again I am a classic dork when it comes to meeting famous people. For example, I heard my name being called once while standing outside a Santa Monica hotel. I turned around to answer and found myself looking at Sean Penn. Here is the brilliant thing I said to him: "Oh! You're a Shawn, too!"

If *Steady On* was about getting sober, going to therapy, and the end of my relationship with John Leventhal, *Fat City* was about feeling good. I think it was an easier record to make, probably because there was no drama between Larry Klein and me. It was a friendly, warm relationship, and so it was more fun, too.

The song I'd started on the uptown bus to therapy, "Polaroids," opened the album. The rhythm of that song lent itself to a lot of conversation, a lot of words, a lot of visuals. I didn't have an ending, and one night I dreamed of two people in love. They were walking on a plank across a huge gully or a crevasse—and she turned around and held up a card that said "Valentine" while he was taking Polaroids of her. That was it; I knew how to end the song.

Romantically I was inspired by a couple of different men this time around. Remember the nerdy boy who rejected me by feeding the cats and driving me to arson? He was at the core of "Tennessee" and "Monopoly," proving that it doesn't take much to get yourself written into one of my songs.

Musically "Tennessee" was a sort of departure for me. John had written the music, and it was more rock and roll than anything I'd tried to write before. Richard Thompson graced us with a screaming guitar solo, and Béla Fleck played a nasty banjo part—you don't see the words "nasty" and "banjo" together very often, but Béla does things with a banjo that are rather unusual, to say the least.

I wrote "Round of Blues" for my new love (not the perv), an Englishman, Simon Tassano. Simon was lithe and light, with golden skin and hair, the bluest eyes, the loveliest mouth, a beautiful man. I bought him a silver sun on a beaded silver chain because he was Sunny Simon, always cheerful. In the early days, I started to fall in love with him upon hearing him sing Joni Mitchell songs, badly. Simon is a thoroughly charming, easygoing master of the soundboard and peerless caretaker for Richard Thompson, with whom I toured America and Europe in 1991. I was still promoting *Steady On*, and Richard was promoting his album, *Rumor and Sigh*. I would open the show each night, then play rhythm guitar and sing backup in Richard's band during his set. To this day this tour stands out as one of my favorites ever. I worked my ass off, had the time of my life playing with and learning from Richard, who is simply brilliant, and fell in love with Simon. Who was engaged. But not to me.

Richard Thompson tour, Newport, RI, 1991

Every tour should come with a warning about falling in love while on the road. (And if you tour Europe, the warning should be in large red capital letters.) It isn't real life. It's fairly simple out there, romantically so, breezing in and out from one city to the next, one's only actual responsibility being to show up and play each night, which is a pleasure. Of course you're working, but it is really about pleasure: the pleasure of playing, the pleasure of camaraderie, the pleasure of food and sleep and entertainment—and love affairs. We resisted each other for as long as we could, until I told him I'd be willing to have a relationship with him for the duration of the tour, no questions asked, no expectations. I'm not normally capable of such compartmentalization, but he was so dear and it made me so happy to be near him. I didn't see him as a philanderer, just a guy stuck in a moment that he couldn't get out of. Somewhere along the way, I think it was in western Canada, he told me he was falling for me. I was wearing a black dress with a golden sun on the front, lent to me by my friend Elly Brown. Now we had a problem. Ultimately, Simon made the decision to break off his engagement in order to pursue a relationship with me, and I was glad, although in hindsight, with a few more heartbreaks under my belt, I truly regret the pain I brought into his fiancée's life. But we were in love; it was a runaway train. Backstage at a gig in Cornwall, England, I wrote the first lines to "Round of Blues." It's Simon's song.

Simon and me, Sydney, Australia, 1992

During the making of *Fat City,* I went with Simon to visit his son in Australia. I remember camping with Simon and Tom, looking at the stars and finding Orion. It was a romantic notion to me that we could all see that same constellation, no matter where we were, even with thousands and thousands of miles separating us. When I got back to L.A., I took a lush piece of music that Larry had given me and began "Orion in the Sky."

Because of Simon there are some other affirmative love songs on *Fat City,* like "Climb on a Back That's Strong" and "Object of My Affection," both of them infused with hope and promise, not exactly my forte on *Steady On.*

Recording with Larry meant using an entirely different group of musicians than those on *Steady On.* We had David Lindley, whose solo on "Polaroids" still makes me cry. I especially wanted to use the Subdudes, a rootsy outfit from New Orleans who reminded me of the Band. They played on "Object of My Affection" and "Tenderness on the Block," a cover of a tune by Warren Zevon and Jackson Browne—which was also up-tempo and hopeful! (What was in the Kool-Aid??) I'd written a song with Elly Brown called "Set the Prairie on Fire," and Larry brought in Booker T. Jones to play a sultry organ part, while I asked Chris Whitley, a labelmate and one of my favorite artists, to add some slide guitar. That song also featured Jim Keltner on drums, and I was beyond excited to work with him. We recorded six takes of "Prairie," and Jim never played the same part twice, which is an aspect of his genius. The difficulty was in choosing which drum take was the coolest.

The best surprise when it came to players was certainly Steuart Smith. Steuart plays the guitar with crazy precision and a true, true heart. I'd seen him at the Bottom Line in New York accompanying Rosanne Cash, and I remember telling him afterward that I couldn't stop smiling when he played. There was this whole incestuous minidrama going on where Rosanne was now dating, and working with, John Leventhal, I was working with Steuart, and Larry had just finished producing an album by Rodney Crowell, Rosanne's ex-husband, using Steuart and John on guitar. Yikes. But I felt so lucky to have found Steuart, who in addition to being an amazing guitar player is one of the smartest, funniest, most passionate, sincere, and hardworking people I've ever met. Nowadays Steuey is an Eagle, and I'm still mad at Don Henley for stealing him, but who can blame him? Steuart rocks.

Larry Klein turned what seemed like a horribly daunting prospect—making music without John Leventhal—into a joy. When we finished up *Fat City*, it was time to go on tour again. I got the late, great T-Bone Wolk to play bass, Jeff Young on keyboards, Kenny Blevins on drums, and Steuart on guitar. I was still with a bunch of boys, but this time I had a bus! My first-ever bus tour. I can still remember pulling in to a town, getting off the bus in my uniform of a pair of men's striped pajamas, and going into a radio station for an early-morning drive-time interview.

Simon defected from Richard long enough to run the tour and do the sound. I fared considerably better during this outing than on my previous one, what with having a boyfriend, a bus, a band, *and* Prozac. I'd learned what I could and couldn't do vocally, although we did a cover of "Look Out Cleveland" that I'm pretty sure didn't do the song justice. We opened the show with "Dead of the Night" and did this little medley of "Tracks of My Tears" into "Cry Like an Angel." I had a blast.

There was just one problem in my life now: Simon lived in London, I lived in New York. We both figured that all we really needed was a nearby airport, and beyond that we were wide open. So we did the only reasonable thing two people in love can do—we moved to L.A.

14
You Always Knew It

The Masters of Rhythm and Taste, Italy, 1993

This is my window to the world.

Simon and I settled in Los Angeles, and I had an idea for my next record. I figured for all the cover tunes I'd learned and played all those years, I ought to record some of them, and besides, I just hadn't written much since *Fat City*. I decided to ask Steuart Smith to produce. The record was called, aptly enough, *Cover Girl*—title courtesy of Simon.

"Every Little Thing She Does Is Magic," which opens the record, was one of the first songs I learned that represented a departure from all the singer-songwriter material I'd been covering since I was fifteen. I played it in the Bleecker Street days in the mid- to late 1980s. I learned Tom Waits's "Heart of Saturday Night" up in the attic in Berkeley, 1979. Dylan's "You're Gonna Make Me Lonesome When You Go" is another from that time period. I'd gotten deep, deep into "Blood on the Tracks," and I swore I'd wrestle a melody out of that song. The Talking Heads' "This Must Be the Place (Naive Melody)" is a cover I'm really proud of. After listening closely to the lyrics, I discovered the sweetest love song inside their perky, bouncy arrangement.

There were two fairly obscure songwriters that I was keen to record—Willis Alan Ramsey and Judee Sill. The covers of these two songs—"Satin Sheets" and "There's a Rugged Road," respectively—are truer to the original artists' versions simply because they *are* obscure, and I wanted to represent the originals. Willis Alan Ramsey put out one record in his life. I learned about it when I moved to Austin, in 1976. Everybody in Austin knew about Willis. It's one of the best records I've ever heard—a desert-island disc. I even got to see Willis play a couple of times in Austin in the seventies—and that era is gone. He's missed.

Judee Sill was my own discovery. I was still in high school and scooping ice cream at Baskin-Robbins. We had a college radio station, WTAO; we played that in the ice-cream store. A song came on called "There's a Rugged Road." I just stopped what I was doing. The singer was a woman, an acoustic guitar, and then these otherworldly, heavenly harmonies come in on the chorus. I was able to track it down to Judee's album *Heart Food*. She made two records, and I love every song on both.

Steve Earle says the fact that I recorded his song "Someday" made a difference to him at that time in his life. I never will feel like I came close to touching his version, but I was obsessed with that song, and if it meant something to Steve, then I can go on living.

As I mentioned earlier, one of the artists who really taught me the most about relating to an audience, and about being a performer and a songwriter, was Greg Brown, one of the first artists I ever opened for, back at Passim. I'd always loved his tune "One Cool Remove" and liked the idea of doing it with my friend Mary Chapin Carpenter. I also covered the Band, Jimmy Webb, and "Killin' the Blues"—that has-no-rhymes gem by Roly Salley from my days with Buddy—and a great song called "Window to the World" by a Tennessee band called the Questionnaires, led by Tom Littlefield. Tom and I co-wrote a song called "Trouble" that I would record on my next album.

This was a full, joyous time in my life. Simon and I got married in 1993 in the desert out at Twentynine Palms in Joshua Tree National Park. I'd now made three records. Tours were launched for both *Fat City* and *Cover Girl,* and Simon managed and did sound for them. I'd finally gotten used to that aspect of my job; in fact, I was more than used to it—I was loving it. Larry Klein, Steuart Smith, and I formed a trio for the road, and it was the best band I ever had.

We called ourselves the Masters of Rhythm and Taste, and we were a lean, mean outfit. I'd never felt so at home musically. There was just enough sound, and every note and beat counted; there was no fat to trim, no drums to sing over—Steuart said we were wearing drummer repellent. The essence of each song had to be captured by just the three of us, and to my ears we sounded fuller than an entire orchestra. There was magic and mojo among me and Steuart and Larry, both onstage and off. We were friends and bandmates, a perfect little microcosm of artistic and social heaven. I was with Simon, so the likelihood of road-induced hanky-panky was nil. The three of us were tightly bonded through our love of music, of course—and a thoroughly sick sense of humor

The aforementioned Rudy Ray Moore *Zodiac* tape was required listening on the bus, post-show. I can't even quote it here—it's just too blue—but it decompressed us and set the stage for whatever movie we might decide to watch. And watch repeatedly. Steuart and Larry were fans of *The Bad Lieutenant,* a Harvey Keitel film so depraved it was barely watchable. I preferred a PBS special called *The Donner Party,* a perky documentary about cannibalism. Thereafter Steuart referred to our backstage cold cuts as "Donner party platters." While watching *Alien,* Steuart had the bright idea of slowing the film down frame by frame just at the moment the creature shoots out of the egg and attaches itself to John Hurt's face. He claimed that it was all done with raw chicken.

Steuart was extremely picky about movies; his guru was *New Yorker* film critic Pauline Kael. We all loved Martin Scorsese. *Raging Bull* and *Goodfellas* were staples on the bus. (I met Ray Liotta one time and asked him to please say, "Karen," just once. He did.) I brought *The Last Waltz* and *Casino. Casino* might not have been as perfect as some other Scorsese films, but it has that great Scorsese rhythm along with a killer sound track. About a quarter of the way through it one night on the bus, Steuey, who'd had a little wine, stood up, slammed down his glass, and muttered, as he stomped back to his bunk, "It's sloppy, it's mean-spirited, and it's *shit*." It may have been when Joe Pesci stabbed a guy in the neck with a fountain pen.

About midpoint during our show every night, Larry and Steuart would go offstage so I could do a couple of songs by myself. I had a standard joke that I would tell about their having to leave the stage to be treated by the medical staff because they were drug addicts. I explained that I was a responsible employer and wouldn't force them to go out on the street to satisfy their habit. One night while I was saying this, Steuart rode a bicycle behind me across the stage.

Before we went on each night, Larry would pull me aside. He would solemnly take my hand, turn it over, and put his finger in my palm. "Shawny-Shawn-Shawn. Here," he began, "here is the audience. You must put them here. And then"—and as he said this, he would subtly tilt my hand from side to side—"you must play with them. You must always give them something," he would say, "but do not give them everything." At a small club in Italy, we once did a thankless, awkward show where only members of the press were invited. Most of them didn't speak English, and I wager most of them didn't want to be there. I was tired, and I was not in the mood. When we went on, I stood very still and closed my eyes, never opening them once throughout the entire performance, giving probably the most lackluster show ever. Backstage afterward, Larry threw up his hands in mock despair and wailed, "But you must give them *something*!"

Larry's alter ego was "Señor de la Noche," which loosely translated means "Lord of the Night." In a former life, while working with some Latin jazz players in the eighties, he was so christened during all-night cocaine binges. Señor de la Noche would appear to us from time to time, to say in a thick Spanish accent, "I know exactly what you mean, my man." Or, when particularly nostalgic, he might sigh wistfully, "Ahhh, *la cocaína*— the laaady . . ." Señor was a bit of a prankster as well, often daring us, for a reward of "two hundred pesos," to confront total strangers about their clothing or hair or sexual habits, usually in airports when we were forced to abandon our beloved bus and fly. When that was the case, Steuart, who loathed flying, would ingest a concoction he called his "atta-boy cocktail": a tranquilizer, Ativan, washed down with a martini. Or two. After a long flight from L.A. to Melbourne, Steuart emerged from the plane completely disheveled and asked in all seriousness, with just a hint of panic, "Does anyone else feel upside down?" Señor de la Noche wearily replied, of course, "I know *exactly* what you mean, my man."

One of the great friends I made in California was David Mirkin, who loves music more than anyone else I know, except maybe Steuart. Dave can tell you not only who sings lead on any Beatles song, he can tell you who breathed where. Dave is divinely funny, ridiculously so, and is responsible for launching my cool factor into the stratosphere by getting me to voice a character on *The Simpsons*, which he executive-produces. I was Rachel Jordan, a Christian rock singer. It was also Dave who got Garry Shandling to come down to my gig one night. Garry asked if I would appear on his series, and that's how I got on *The Larry Sanders Show*.

Meanwhile, despite the fun things I was doing and the good friends I was making, I had to wonder what had possessed me to relocate to California. Yes, of course I loved the flea markets, a shopaholic's true nirvana, but if you're from the Midwest, you just can't feel at home without a good thunderstorm now and then, and they didn't exist in L.A. And, of course, there was the Northridge earthquake in 1994. Our friend, Danny Ferrington, an ace guitar maker who hails originally from Louisiana and has a voice registering somewhere between those of Minnie Mouse and James Carville, took this opportunity to defend his gas-guzzling SUV, saying, "When the shit hits the fan like this, I can get home!" Meaning he could off-road down Lincoln Drive to his apartment in the Palisades. I did everything wrong during that earthquake. As soon as the house started pitching like a washing machine at 4:00 A.M., I ran directly to the back door and panicked. Not recommended. Then I ran to the front door screaming while every car alarm for miles went off. That seismic party, along with the lack of weather in L.A., put me over the edge.

I had a gig in Austin and decided to look for a house there. Simon was on board for the move. Austin was a music town and had great food, no earthquakes, and no shortage of thunderstorms. In no time flat, I found my dream home, really just a *Leave It to Beaver* house but *right across the street* from Lake Austin, with a *boat dock* to boot. I threw my down payment at it, and we loaded up the truck and moved to Scenic Drive—yes, that was the name of my street. Scenic bloody Drive. Oh, Lord, oh, Lord, why in the name of God did I ever sell that house? You don't sell a house on Scenic Drive; you hold on to it for dear life so you can retire in ten years. Simon went on tour with Richard Thompson, and there I was, sitting in a four-bedroom mortgage. The house on Scenic Drive turned out to be a house of cards.

15
Sunny Came Home

Julie Speed's Setting the World on Fire *oil painting*

Line 'em up in a row.
Gunshot—ready, set, go.

During our first few months in Austin, I sat with a bunch of guitars and notebooks in my "writing room," which was actually just a bedroom upstairs overlooking the water. I'd gaze out at the lake, trying to take in my good luck. I'd never had a writing room before. Shouldn't I be prolific and brilliant now that I did? It was no use. When I write, I like to empty my mind and focus in on a feeling or a rhythm or a melody. But my head was spinning. Why, oh, why had I moved away from New York, a hotbed of edge and sophistication and artiness where a weird South Dakota girl like me seemed downright normal? What was I doing in a neighborhood living among doctors and lawyers with no Korean delis, no Two Boots Pizza, no MoMA? Where I had to *drive* to get anywhere? How could I have left my crazy friends, Stokes and Kim? Oh, I stared at that lake and came up empty. I was neck-deep in the biggest commitment I'd ever undertaken, becoming a homeowner. Wedding vows were cake compared to this. There was nothing to do but write about it: "Go jump in the lake, / Go ride up the hill, / Get out of this house." Yes, the starting point for my next album was inspired by buyer's remorse, and it would take down my marriage.

It's rather glib of me to blame the failure of my relationship with Simon on a house, but the bottom line is that I wasn't ready for either of them, the husband or the house, and it certainly wasn't the first time, nor would it be the last, that I ran from commitment.

We'd had our troubles even in California. Simon liked his pot, and I wasn't woman enough to just let him. It irritated me when he became stoned and got dry mouth and talked slowly and acted spacey and giggled over nothing. One night at a party in L.A., he wandered off for a while, and I knew it was demon pot that got him. Sure enough, he returned to where I was sitting in the garden, and I was grossed out. Seeing my boyfriends in altered states threatened me; I wanted to be able to relate to them at all times. Of course I could have attempted a little sense memory from back in my druggie days, but I didn't. I was annoyed, and Simon agreed to leave the party and call it a night. As I drove us home, I felt a little sheepish for coming down on him and suggested we rent a movie. He agreed apprehensively, not sure if he liked me, but then slowly his whole face lit up. Still foggy and silly from the reefer, he exclaimed, "Oh! Could we get a comedy?" We got Monty Python, a stoned Englishman's nirvana.

But we'd had lovely times, too. In the L.A. days, Simon rewrote the words to the Crowded House song "Weather with You":

Walkin' round the room in my favorite sweater
At 209 Rennie Avenue.
It's the same gear, but everything's different.
We got a garden and a bar-b-que.
Kay is cookin' in our kitchen,
Jane's Addiction on the radio,
Caesar salad at the Souplantation,
Simon and Larry say, "Oh, nooo."

My sister, Kay, had lived not far down the road from us in Venice. She worked as a sound tech on films. We became addicted to the Souplantation, an all-you-can-eat cornucopia of salads and soups. We would stuff ourselves there and went so often that Simon began to dread dinnertime. Twice we went to Australia to visit Simon's son, Tom. Fond, fond memories. Simon was a love. He still is. Just last summer Callie and I took him and Tom out on Lake Austin for the day.

But back then I felt trapped and completely out of my depth at the prospect of committing to forever and building true intimacy. I found that living with someone wasn't something I could put my best self into. I felt suffocated. I didn't like sharing or compromising. Simply put, I was childish. The thrill of the chase and getting married had worn off, and, of course, some real issues came to light, both his and mine. I found myself unwilling and unable to work them out, and so between the husband and the house, I kept the house and fled the man by asking Simon to move out. We had been married two years.

It was back to the writing room, or the drawing room, or even the rubber room perhaps. At any rate, I hadn't made a record of original material in almost four years. The folks at Passim would surely not approve. It was time.

I had written a few fragments of music and lyrics and had finished two whole songs, "If I Were Brave" and "New Thing Now." But I needed help to write more material, and it occurred to me that maybe enough water had gone under the bridge for John and me to take a stab at writing again. We hadn't worked together in five years and probably hadn't spoken in three, which allowed me to get some distance and move on both personally and musically. I called him one day in 1994, and the next thing I knew, he had flown down to Austin to meet with me.

The tension between us was gone. We could actually be friends. I was less self-conscious around him, having realized I could work without him and having finally moved on past the wreckage of our romance. John and I no longer felt obligated to consider Top 40 radio in our efforts. I'd compromised before, re-mixing and re-producing songs like "I Don't Know Why" on *Fat City* and "Every Little Thing She Does Is Magic" on *Cover Girl* against my better judgment for the sole purpose of getting radio play. It had never worked. In fact, when John and I reunited, all we were hoping for was a little inspiration and spark musically, like in the good old days. I remember both of us feeling as though we had nothing to prove. To anybody, not even each other, or perhaps least of all each other. As near as I can tell, that made all the difference.

It was as though the stars had aligned. Anything went, we

weren't precious about it. We pushed each other without try-ing—I went after melodies and lyrics in unusual ways, and John was coming up with amazing pieces and fleshing out wonderful production ideas. I didn't care about singing perfectly, and he didn't care about pristine production. On *Steady On*, you'd have thought we were curing cancer. I guess we had both grown up a little—after all, it wasn't rocket science. It was *fun*.

The writing was magically easy. He had a piece that I called "Get Out of This House," a rocker, and I basically just threw words at it. I adopted a pissed-off attitude and improvised on tape, filling in lines on paper as I went. I wanted to sound like I didn't care about the singing, only the attitude. This was new.

John suggested we try to write something similar to a Crowded House song that I played live, called "Private Universe." When in doubt, steal, we always say, and steal from the best. As we messed around with chord changes, I was looking through my notebook and had the idea to take lyrics I'd written in 1993 with Tom Littlefield (who wrote "Window to the World" on *Cover Girl*) and insert them into the song. I tried them with this new melody, new chord changes, and a different time signature. After a few weeks, it all came together, and we had "Trouble." That's what I call our mash-up method.

I used my speaking-in-tongues technique on "You and the Mona Lisa." I took John's music and sang nonsense syllables, and the phrase "you and the Mona Lisa" came out of my mouth. I had no idea what it meant at that point, but I just decided to follow the words. At the beginning of the song, I sang "Hoist a pint, to the lads" for a good long time before I finally found the right words—"nothing in particular." In fact, I sang the whole song as a drunk British sailor for a bit, but in the end it wasn't what we were after. Thankfully. Words can let you know what the song is about before you even consciously realize it.

The lyrics turned out to be based on my little niece Grace.

These days when I play the song, I'll give the audience an update on Grace, who at this writing is fifteen and recently shaved her head.

"Wichita Skyline" was a total combo of stealing, speaking in tongues, mashing, and cheating. The music John wrote had a low, twangy guitar break, an obvious ode to "Wichita Lineman," one of the best songs in the whole world. And I knew I wanted the lyrical imagery to evoke the Great Plains of South Dakota, where I grew up. I thought, what would Bob Dylan do? And suddenly I thought of *Nashville Skyline*. So I had my title, "Wichita Skyline," although I meant to change it to be more specific to South Dakota. The word "Wichita" sings so nicely, though, and honestly, the only other town name I could come up with that scanned as well as "Wichita" was "Tokyo," and that obviously wouldn't do. I cheated by getting out a map and borrowing the towns of Independence, Missouri, and Salina, Kansas, which I pronounce incorrectly in the song, but there was a good reason! A storm blows in on the last verse, and the singer looks up at the sky to find "a patch of blue." There was a movie called *A Patch of Blue* with Sydney Poitier and Shelley Winters—a wretchedly heartbreaking movie; I loved it—with a character named Selina, played by Elizabeth Hartman, an abused blind girl in the South who falls in love with Sydney Poitier. I stupidly borrowed her name to represent the town of Salina, which is actually pronounced "sal-EYE-na," only I say "sa-LEE-na."

I'd written the lyrics to "The Facts About Jimmy." John just threw a guitar piece at me later. It was a mash-up. "I Want It Back" was something I started on a National steel guitar in G tuning. It was a slight steal from "Cold Blue Steel and Sweet Fire" guitarwise and took its inspiration lyrically from how lost I felt, alone in that Scenic Drive house, trying to write but reading *People* magazine instead and balking at celebrity worship.

"If I Were Brave" started on an airplane ride to New Orleans for a gig at Tipitina's. It was one of those great instances where I kind of heard the chord progression and the melody in my head before I even had a chance to put it down, and I knew as well that it would be on piano. Very simple piano, which is all I'm capable of. It was one of those gifts where the essence of the song, at least musically, was apparent to me. "If I Were Brave" was about my failed marriage to Simon and all the questions I was asking myself about what I could have done to make it work, including having a child. I wrote most of it on that plane ride.

The album closer, "Nothin' on Me," was the one song that survived out of all the things John and I had written back in the horn-rimmed-pop days. It ended up on the record partially because of the record company's hope that it could become a hit. I was glad to do the song; it was fun, it had swagger, I enjoyed the lyrics, but it did not become a hit. It did, however, become the opening theme song for the TV sitcom *Suddenly Susan*, starring Brooke Shields, that ran in the late nineties.

"Sunny Came Home" didn't start as the story of a tortured housewife's revenge. John had given me a fully produced piece of music to write melody and lyrics to. Originally I called it "40 Red Men," a clever way, I thought, to talk about my loathsome daily habit of smoking two packs of red-box Marlboro cigarettes. Needless to say, the words "forty red men" didn't sing very well, and, as my A&R man said, "I don't think anyone is going to care about forty red men. Besides, it sounds like you're referring to Native Americans, and then you'll be in a world of shit."

So at the last minute I had to back up and rewrite the song to complete the record. I had already chosen the cover art, a painting by my friend Julie Speed. Her subjects were often women on the verge. I could relate. For example, there was a portrait of a rather sweet, peaceful woman with little flames on top of her head, like a crown, and the title was *Please Help Me, My Brain Is Burning*. I chose for the cover a classic Julie-scape with a woman in the foreground of a vast, flat prairie, holding a lit match. Wasn't that me, really, a girl setting the prairie on fire? Far, far in the distance, on the horizon, there was a very large fire. Although the title, *A Few Small Repairs,* belonged to an entirely different piece, a collage of a woman sewn and safety-pinned together, Julie was all for mixing and matching titles, and when we applied *A Few Small Repairs* to the fiery landscape painting, the effect was, to us, a riot. Whatever repairs that woman was making were neither few nor small.

In an actual moment of marketing wisdom, of which I generally possess very little, I decided to finish that last song by making it about the woman in the painting. I called her Sunny, wove in the line "it's time for a few small repairs," and the record was done. I called it—what else?—*A Few Small Repairs.*

The timing couldn't have been better. It was 1996, and Lilith Fair was about to take off. Columbia decided it was time to really pull the trigger on me and threw all their weight into the marketing of *A Few Small Repairs.* First they released "Get Out of This House" as a single, and it achieved modest success. Then they released "Sunny." I don't remember what radio station played it first, or even how far up the charts it went. I'd already made and promoted three records without any singles catching on, and I really wasn't paying attention. I do remember the head of radio at Columbia, Charlie Walk, calling once as the song gained more and more airplay and crowing, "Sunny's comin' home, baby!" I just laughed. But then things started to happen that made me aware that something exciting was going on with "Sunny Came Home."

Larry and Steuart and I were touring with Lilith during the summer of 1997 when "Sunny" was released. Our slot was in the late afternoon, and while we were certainly featuring songs from *A Few Small Repairs,* we weren't being dogged about it. We'd play "Sunny" somewhere in the middle of the set. But after a few weeks, we noticed that whenever we played that particular song, we were seeing the quintessence of a true rock-and-roll audience in top form, with lighters ablaze and arms waving. And right at the end of the song, during the instrumental outro, the roar would start. I'd seen enough concerts to know I had to make the song the last one in the set and milk that response for all it was worth. As we took our bow one evening, Steuart, a purist who eschewed any form of idolatry, turned to me while we were upside down and said, "I like this." Yes. I'd made a video for "Sunny Came Home" as well, and in the food court of a mall in Indianapolis, a high-school basketball player looked at me and said to his friends, "Hey, there's Sunny!" And that, ladies and gentlemen, is what I call fame. I think the song made it to number one, but I knew it was big when the audiences at Lilith Fair waved their lighters, and because of that kid in Indy.

Receiving my gold record, 1996

And I did my own tour with a band including Steuart, Doug Petty on keyboards, Alison Prestwood on bass, Kate Markowitz on vocals, and Chris Searles on drums. Then the Grammy nominations were announced. Yes, "Sunny" had been a hit, but I was floored—John and I were up for two of the biggest awards, Record of the Year and Song of the Year.

The nominations represented to me a measure of success that was very special. There was never any question about wanting my mother and father to be part of it, and I flew them to New York for the show. They'd witnessed enough scenes with me that hadn't gone so well. This was different, to say the least. Mom and I got our makeup and hair done in the hotel. And then we all drove to the ceremony in a white limo. The mood was upbeat and giddy. It was enough just to be going, win or lose. It really was. Nothing could have dampened our spirits.

At the Grammys, Radio City Music Hall, January 1998, John and I were backstage, having just performed "Sunny Came Home." And then we heard our names being called: we'd won Song of the Year. We only made it a few steps onstage, though, when our moment of glory was hijacked. Ol' Dirty Bastard from Wu-Tang Clan chose this particular moment to storm the stage and rant about not having won an award earlier that night. He was shaking his fists and yelling—about what, we had no idea, because we couldn't understand a word, being behind him. The only thing I could decipher was, "Wu-Tang is for the children!" John's and my disparate reactions to this event perfectly describe the difference in our general attitudes. I thought, *Oh, God, what did I do wrong?* whereas John was thinking, *Boy, this guy really loves our stuff!*

The next day I received the biggest bouquet of flowers from Ol' Dirty Bastard with a note that read, *"Sorry for messing up your night, Love, Ol' Dirty Bastard."* That's something not just anyone can lay claim to.

Other crazy things happened during the ceremony: A fellow with the words SOY BOMB written on his torso managed to get onstage while Bob Dylan was performing. We all thought he was promoting alternative energy until someone pointed out that perhaps he was trying to say, "I am the bomb," in Spanish. And then a hydraulically lifted stage set piece began to rise from the floor as Vanessa Williams was walking out, nearly cutting her in half.

Later that evening there were all sorts of festivities, naturally, but what stands out in my mind is meeting Bob Dylan. I was led to a VIP room—I had come by it honestly that night—and there he was, sitting at a table between Cyndi Lauper and Diana Ross. We were introduced, and he took my hand, bent over, and meant to kiss it, I guess, but it really was more like he wiped his nose on it. I'll never care, though. Put any kind of Dylan DNA on me, I'm good.

What I've always said about winning a Grammy Award is that there isn't one bad thing about it. It looks great on the résumé and is super helpful in convincing your parents and your past teachers, especially fifth-grade English ones who once deemed your poetry "trite and sugary," that you aren't a lost cause after all. Did I think we would win? Given the competition—which included Hanson, R. Kelly, Sheryl Crow, Paula Cole, Diane Warren, and Gwen Stefani—I sure didn't think we were a shoo-in. "Sunny Came Home" had done well but I was hardly a superstar. Still, ever since Bonnie Raitt swept the awards in 1990 for *Nick of Time* at age forty-one, it seemed as if anything was possible.

John and I won two Grammy Awards that night. One for Record of the Year. And Song of the Year—that's for *songwriting.* Bonnie, it just got better. *And* I was carrying around a little something extra that night. Guess who's coming to dinner? And breakfast and lunch? For the next eighteen years?

The big night, 1998

16
Hold on Tight

Me and Mario Erwin, baby daddy, 1996

I believe I have pulled a major coup.
I believe I have boarded up the zoo.
I believe I have dropped the other shoe.
And there's nothing like you.

In 1996, just as I finished *A Few Small Repairs,* I met Mario Erwin, a freelance photographer–turned–graphics salesman for a local Austin outfit. A mutual friend and her fiancé introduced us at the lake. Mario was going to take us all waterskiing. Although he hailed from Arkansas, he was of Italian descent and had lovely olive skin and big, bright, blue eyes. He was compact and sinewy, like my father, and his style was no-bullshit, wry, sarcastic. I hadn't dated in about a year, and when I met Mario, I thought, *Well, I could sleep with this guy.* He called the next day and asked if we could go to dinner and did I want to go tomorrow or the following weekend? "The sooner the better," I said. "We might as well find out if we like each other."

We liked each other. In fact, Mario announced to me that same week that he liked everything about me—shouldn't we be an item? It sounded good to me. I was lonesome. This might have been the right time for me to have played the field, but I'll tell you, that concept eludes me. I don't get it. Does that make me a serial monogamist? Or just a one-man woman? I even tried to suggest we not be exclusive right at first, sensing that my habit of diving headfirst into romances within minutes might be a problem. But Mario wouldn't have it. I was flattered, I liked being wanted, and I was only too happy to be tied down. Mario had a boat. I had a dock. After a couple of dates, he put his boat in my dock—and yes, I get the symbolism.

My niece Grace was about a year old by then. I was in love with that child; I even felt partial ownership. And part of me felt lacking. I was the older sister, and Kay had taken the leap into motherhood first. Well, damn it, if she could do it, so could I.

I'd always had a difficult time picturing myself as a mother. I spent a great deal of my life resenting my folks for all their failings as I saw them. Part of me thought I could best them in the parent department, and part of me knew I had set impossibly high standards. I didn't have pets because I traveled too much. I couldn't keep a plant alive. I liked that I could spend an entire day if I wanted to just hiding from the world. Before I got sober at age twenty-seven, I was basically surviving. Afterward I began to be comfortable in my own skin. I could viscerally feel myself making up for lost time. I loved choosing what I would eat, loved that I had my own coffeepot, my own bed, my own apartment. I took myself to movies, things like that. Simple pleasures, more peace, fewer voices.

Fast-forward several years down the road. I'd had my fill of what eventually felt like a selfish lifestyle, and I remember thinking that if I were to have balance I was either going to have to have a child or devote myself to a cause. Something in me yearned to give. And meeting Mario and Grace almost simultaneously sent my biological clock into Oh. Ver. Drive. I'd made records, I'd traveled the world, I'd already been married once, and I was forty. It was now or never. When I got off tour at the end of the summer in 1996, Mario presented me with a back porch he had built himself onto the house on Scenic Drive, along with a diamond ring. We got married October 19, 1997, and by Thanksgiving I was pregnant.

Pregnant at Lilith Fair, June 1998

On the heels of *A Few Small Repairs,* the record company asked me to do a Christmas record. I couldn't see my way clear to making sense of the idea until I remembered a book I'd been given when I was eight years old. It was called *Lullabies and Night Songs.* And while they weren't Christmas songs, I thought I could probably blend those lullabies with lullaby-like Christmas songs, given that Christmas is about a baby being born and all. There was something in the way Alec Wilder voiced these songs for the piano. They reminded me of Aaron Copland. Beautiful and odd. It was summer, and I was eight and a half months pregnant when I recorded *Holiday Songs and Lullabies.* We made it in Austin with my keyboard player, Doug Petty, producing. Doug had owned the same book as a kid. The morning of July 24, 1998, I went into labor, and our daughter was born ten hours later, at 6:00 P.M., with "A Whiter Shade of Pale" playing in the background.

We took her home after only one night in the hospital—I was anxious to be a "real" mother. On *A Few Small Repairs,* I had a song called "If I Were Brave" where I asked, "Would I be saved, if I were brave and had a baby?" Well, yes and no. There is no rescue as I once imagined it, no secret answer, no one safe place. I think it's the being brave that saves us, maybe. Is it brave to have a baby? Oh, without a doubt.

When did I know that postpartum depression had set in? I was overwhelmed, teary, completely thrown by this stranger in my house who required my constant attention, up to and including latching itself onto part of my body for nourishment. Does anyone talk about this, really? It isn't that I didn't love her or couldn't bond with her. I felt deep empathy and responsibility for her and cared with all my heart. But I was awfully scared and unfamiliar with everything that was asked of me as the mother of a newborn. Life as I knew it was over—it was that simple. There were no off hours or holidays with which to be completely selfish. As one of my sister's friends said, "You'll never sleep the same way again." Nothing would ever be the same again. My body and even my face looked different. The sky, the trees, the very air I breathed seemed to change.

A month after the baby was born, which seemed like an eternity, I got to go out with my sister. It was my first outing since the birth. Neil Finn of Crowded House was in town. We tracked down Neil and his wife, Sharon, at a restaurant. I must've looked like a deer in the headlights, because Sharon took my hand and told me that Neil's brother, Tim, had just become a father. "Oh, wonderful, how are they doing?" I asked with false gaiety. "They're shattered," she said, and I felt the utmost gratitude and relief. Someone told the truth. A newborn baby is a terrifying thing to own. It seems to me only those with the most superior emotional upbringings or those who are just blessed with the gift of nurturing can make the transition into parenthood easily.

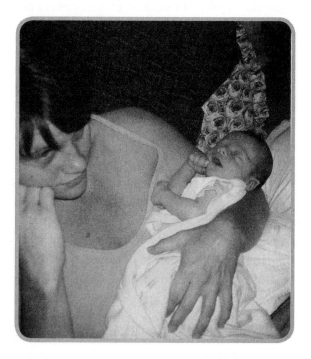

Callie at two days old, July 26, 1998

And the colic—oh, the colic. My sister came over one day early on and gave me the official diagnosis. The baby cried a lot. I could soothe her, but only if I balled her up in the sling, put my little finger in her mouth to suck on, and walked. And I don't mean around the house. I had to go outside. It was August in Austin. I might as well still have been pregnant, given her proximity to my body. The sweat would pour down my face and mix with the tears as I racked up the miles in our neighborhood. She would stop crying, and I would trudge along like a soldier. She would have no part of a baby carriage or a stationary swing or a vibrating seat or a cradle. She wanted back in, basically, and I didn't blame her. I wanted her back in, too. We weren't ready for this. She didn't nap for long stretches, and she ate like a horse. At least that's one thing I knew I was doing right—she was getting fat. I was just *staying* fat. Deep down I wondered if I had made a mistake. I had buyer's remorse again. I like loopholes and return clauses and escape hatches. She didn't come with any of those. I had wanted her more than anything, but when she really became mine, I freaked out. I didn't know how to live in service to anyone else. I had lived for myself up until then. I did what I wanted, got what I wanted. And I knew there was something fundamentally empty about the way I was living. When push came to shove, though, now that the deed was done, I was dubious. Mario had had kids before. He told me that he used to look at me before she was born, all glowing with pregnancy and promise, and think, *She hasn't got a clue.* He was right.

I adjusted. What could I do? I became her mother. I named her Caledonia, because I wanted to call her Cal—after Calpurnia in *To Kill a Mockingbird,* after Cal in *East of Eden,* after the song "Caldonia." She became Callie. I barely worked for her first year, and we got to know each other. She was mine, and I was not going to fuck it up. She breast-fed until she was two and a half, and the only thing that finally put an end to it was the day she held my nipple like a cigar between her back teeth à la Groucho Marx, looked up at me, grinned, and said, "There's a hair on it." I weaned her that day. Her first word was "Dada." Mario took it upon himself to peer into her face and repeat, "Dadadadada- dada," ad nauseam, and it worked, by God.

Her daddy taught me how to burp her—I patted her gently while she fussed after a feeding, and he, having had two other children, grabbed her, threw her over his shoulder, and gave her back a few good whacks. She belched immediately and was happy as a clam. Her daddy fed her, changed her, bathed her, read to her, took her to the park, put her to bed. He gave her language she still uses: "I'm confuzzled," she'll say, or, when not quite up to snuff, "I've got dibucus of the blowhorn today." When I ask her to pick up her stuff, she says, "Make me, punk." That's her dad.

He shops with her and tells her what colors he thinks suit her, and this means the world to her, coming as it does from "a boy." "I'm in love with that little girl," Mario told me when she was days old. She is my first and only, but Mario has been around that block. Callie can't throw him like she can throw me. He's quick to see the drama and laugh her through it. She calls him "Sir Talksalot."

Mario just called me—I'm out of town working on this book. He wouldn't have bothered me, he said, but something has come up. I'm stricken. Is she all right? Yes, but she now has a boy- friend. (She is twelve.) It's the second day of their relationship, and there's a problem. Some of the other girls have told her he's a jerk, and she told him what they said. Now he won't return her texts. "It's the worst day of her life," Mario says. "I thought you should know." He says they sat and talked about it for a long time, that he told her it didn't matter what other people said, that it was between the two of them. "But," he told her, "I may not be the best person to talk to about this, because, after all, I am a boy. You should call your mother." But she didn't call me. She got herself a boyfriend, and drama ensued within two days (the fruit does not fall far from the tree), but she didn't need to call me. She had her daddy.

Her first food was whipped cream. She walked at ten months; she never crawled. She laughed out loud in her sleep when she was less than two weeks old. They say it's not possible for them to laugh at that age, but she did. When I asked someone about it, I was told, "She was chasing angels." I believe it. She never slept through the night, ever. Not even to this day, I don't think. She talks faster than she can think, and her chatter is punctuated by great, deep gasps in an effort to keep the flow going. It's a sort of irritation to her to have to breathe if she's speaking. When she was four, she announced to me while in the bath one day, "I am in love with my clitoris." After I reprimanded her for farting loudly in a Chinese restaurant, she shot me down by glancing around and saying with a shrug, "It's okay. They speak Chinese." I can only assume she farts in English. At the most unexpected times, she will bury her face in my neck and say, "My mama," and I am always, always amazed by this. Someone calls me "Mama." Indeed, I became someone else.

Caledonia, 2002

Little did I know that the real test for me was going to be writing songs with this new identity and everything that came with it. I'd just had my first hit record, and I followed it up with a baby. Not a smart career move, but I never did care about that. Still, I was aware during the first year of Callie's life that I had to make a follow-up record to *A Few Small Repairs* and that there would be an expectation of making another one that would do well. When we made *AFSR,* we didn't know that it would sell. We just made the best record we were capable of, and that's still all I know how to do. I would lie awake with her, nursing her, putting her to sleep, and think, *What in the hell am I going to write about?*

Lyle Lovett said to me once, "Shawn, if you ever decide to have a kid, don't write a fucking song about it." With apologies to my dear friend Lyle, how could I not? She was this wonderful, terrifying, adorable, maddening, thrilling, and crazy bomb detonated in the middle of my life and my career. I wanted to write about the baby—she was my whole life—but it seemed as if every ounce of good creative energy I had was invested in parenting her. I could not find any poetry for it. Words failed me.

I traveled to New York to work with John. Mario and Callie joined me. That was a nice balance; it was great to have my child there so I didn't have to miss her or worry about her, and I could do my work as well. Things came together. I was no longer depressed. I was no longer looking for the escape hatch. But writing for that album was still torturous. I was stuck. And it was made worse by the fact that *A Few Small Repairs* had been so free and seamless and effortless. I thought we had cracked the code. Ha.

What finally happened was, I gave myself permission to express the fear I was feeling. That was the taboo part, and it was keeping me stuck. During that first year, I had such an urge to run away. It's in my personality. I don't like being made to do anything. But it's so wrong to want to run away from your baby—how could I say that? Years before, I had started some lyrics as a love song: "I can pack myself up in a matter of minutes / And leave you all far behind, / All of my old world and

all the things in it are hard to find . . . / If they ever were mine."
I returned to them, and that worked. I could sing about wanting to run but not being able to, chastising myself for having to grow up under the gun, finally. That was the song "Matter of Minutes."

The record is called *Whole New You,* almost called *Bonefields,* but we thought that was too dark. It's a strange, confused, moving piece of work. It was never promoted, and it never sold, and I largely ignore it in my live performances, which is a shame, because there are special songs there. Some, like "One Small Year," I can't even play, because John does it on piano. That one has a line about not knowing my own face, and I meant it literally. "Nothing Like You" is a love song to Callie. So is "I'll Say I'm Sorry Now." "Bound to You" is about the bond between us, "Mr. Levon" about the depression. I've always liked the reference that there is light at times when you are in that state but it's abstract and disoriented, "like California under glass." That's always the way I felt in California, like I was under a glass dome. "Another Plane Went Down" is an eerie journal about the fragility of life.

Alternate cover for Whole New You, *2001*

Whole New You was released on March 27, 2001. It tanked. What a difference four years made. Nobody bought it; hardly anybody heard it. The climate of hit radio had changed completely, and the abundant promo opportunities offered before by Columbia were close to nonexistent. It had been too long—five years—since the previous hit record, and the people at Columbia felt that the material was not going to be radio worthy.

Labels are run less and less these days by music fans and more and more by businesspeople, and the concept of building an artist slowly so he or she will have staying power is being abandoned for signing manufactured acts that can have big hits right out of the chute. There's no room in it for someone like me. I am not your big-hit artist, although I did have a big hit. The climate had changed; it wasn't about women singer-songwriters anymore. That had passed.

In many ways I don't really feel as if I'm in the music business anymore. What I do is kind of archaic. I don't belong at a label that's going to want a million-selling record. That's just not me, and aside from one song and one record, it never really was. I go and play shows with a voice and a guitar, and people come to see me because that is what they want to hear.

Of course, there are great opportunities now that you can have a studio on your iPhone and basically anybody can make a record and put it on the Internet. I think it's pretty cool when I see a commercial and there's this strange song that they just plucked from somewhere and some unknown person gets this big boost. But there is a downside, too. Everything just seems so disposable. I feel I really don't know what's out there. I listen to old stuff. I'm not in touch with what's vital except through Callie sometimes.

With *Whole New You,* my manager met with the president of the label who told him flat-out, "There's nothing I can do with this record." But my manager didn't tell me this until later. I was the last to know. I just slowly figured it out. It was a very bitter pill. Over the course of the next year, I fired my manager, left Columbia, bought a new house, and got divorced. Again.

17
A List of Names

The Manhattan skyline, a bed and a byline.
I've come and I've cradled your face.
And I won't be the last one to commit crimes of passion
With a shoot-out and a chase.

I'm deeply ashamed to have been divorced twice, but not as deeply glad as I am to be divorced. I have a commitment problem and some pesky trust issues that just don't jibe with boy-girl intimacy. It's something I'm learning about myself—I am a loyal friend, a dedicated mother, a dependable colleague, a loving sister and daughter, but I am a lousy girlfriend and an even worse wife.

Here is a list of the men I have found attractive: men who don't want to be with me, men who do want to be with me but can't commit, men who want to be with me but have some fatal flaw, men I don't know, men I know but who refuse to give up fantasies of changing. I seem to yo-yo between blonds and brunettes. If my former boyfriend/husband was blond, then the brunettes have a better shot, and vice versa. Oh, and gray and balding are now copacetic, too. For instance, my last boyfriend was blond and big. My current interest is graying and skinny. I think it's a form of retaliation, of not giving the last one the satisfaction of even thinking I'm trying to replace him. Of course, it's all one big mess of penis envy and Electra complexes, but let's table that for now. I also believe I attempt to shore myself up in the "this one will be different" department by changing the scenery, if you know what I mean. But it's useless, mainly because *I'm* always in the equation, the one constant. There doesn't seem to be any way around that.

As I said to Stokes once, "Why can't I find a man with more than potential?"

You see, at the beginning I want to believe, as all of us do, so much so that I ignore huge red flags. I've discounted sexual addiction, alcoholism, financial improprieties, still being married, homosexuality, toxic narcissism, compulsive lying, and more often than not just your garden-variety bad-boy-dyed-in-the-wool hounddoggishness. Everybody has something, I rationalize.

My song "The Facts About Jimmy" I wrote for someone I never actually dated but was entirely, madly in love with. I believe I'd met him twice, and he jerked my chain a couple of times. He was an absolute dreamboat. He invited me to dinner, and I couldn't believe he might even be interested in me. But ultimately the most that ever happened was that he touched my foot in a hotel room, which I thought was a good start, but there was no follow-up, and I was somewhat bitter. At the time "The Macarena" was at the height of its popularity. You couldn't go anywhere without hearing that song and seeing the accompanying video of two aging Brazilians and their moronic dance. As is the case with all gigantic dance hits, however insipid, once they're in your aural atmosphere, you cannot get rid of them.

One night I was visiting Stokes, and he insisted we watch a pay-per-view video channel and purchase the Macarena—he had succumbed. Stokes is my go-to guy for a man's perspective; he gives it to me straight. After hearing the paltry details of my Jimmy situation, he paused and said, "I don't know why, but for whatever reason he doesn't want to fuck you." Right then and there, I knew what I had to do. I called Jimmy—I didn't know about caller ID yet—and left "The Macarena" on his voice mail so he would be infected with it. Like getting an STD without the sex.

I guess one of my most creative acts of revenge occurred with my second husband, Mario. Callie was itty-bitty brand-new, and I was deep into breast-feeding her. *She* was deep into colic. I tried to keep a record of when she nursed, but it read like Kafka, and I resigned myself to just popping out the breast anytime she yelled, which was constantly. I learned to pump a small village's worth of milk after each feeding so we could freeze it and Mario could handle some of the legwork. One day she just wouldn't eat. I'd give her the breast, and she would latch on and then shake her head like a pit bull. When Mario offered to try the bottle, I was offended. If she didn't want it from the source, why would she want the bottle? He reasoned that he made the bottle milk hot.

"It's coming out of me at ninety-eight point six degrees, for Christ's sake!" I shouted.

"I think I make it a little warmer than that," he countered demurely.

Well, that was it. Knock my mothering any way you want, but don't tell me that my damn breasts are not doing their job. The next morning I took some of the steaming breast milk he had warmed for a feeding, sweetly offered him a cup of coffee, turned my back, and fixed it with breast milk. He never knew the difference.

Lest you think I'm nothing but a retaliatory witch, let me assure you there have been acts of benevolence on my part where men are concerned. I've shown remarkable restraint at times by not calling them in the middle of the night, not calling their new girlfriends in the middle of the night, not calling their best friends in the middle of the night, and not calling their relatives in the middle of the night. Sometimes I have not gone through their wallets or important papers, nor checked their cell phones to see who they've called. I've done my best not to steal or maim their clothing. I think I may have mentioned some issues I have with abandonment and so forth. I am sometimes given to extreme reactions. But mostly in my head. I do know right from wrong; it's just that at times I ignore what I know.

While in relationships I love to jump out of cars. I suppose it's for dramatic effect. Most women can tell you a story about how they jumped out of a car at some point during a fight with their man, most usually while the car was stopped or at least slowing down. Simon and I had a fight while driving from L.A. to Austin when we moved there. I have no earthly idea what it was about, but I ended up stomping around a grassy meridian on I-35 near Waco.

While visiting New Zealand with my last boyfriend, I was involved in another car incident. Our relationship was unfortunate in that he was more of a girl than I was, and there really can't be two divas in the house—it won't work. The man was obsessed with product. He had better hair crème, soap, body lotion, shampoo, conditioner, and face scrub than anyone else I knew. After he broke up with me, he wanted back some lip balm he'd ordered and had had shipped to my house. So I put cat shit in his new trail shoes, which had also been sent to my house after the split, and naturally he was not too happy about that, although I can hardly blame him there. Every girl knows you don't fuck with another girl's shoes.

Anyway, when we arrived in Auckland, my bag didn't show up. This is disastrous in and of itself, but especially when you're meeting your boyfriend's parents for the first time and you've just traveled a trillion miles to do it. We made our connection to Christchurch, got the rental car, and set off to see the folks. Okay, yes, yes, of course New Zealand is beautiful. But it's cold down there. And windy. And all I had were my plane clothes. I was a plane-clothes defective. And I was jet-lagged. And nervous. And Mr. Nancyboy didn't care—he had his bag with his Fresh Sake Hair Cream. I knew I was supposed to feel like Cate Blanchett in *Lord of the Rings*, but in fact I was just in a cold, windy, foreign country, in a car that was on the wrong side of the road. I began to cry, and we pulled over. Get the picture? I hope so, because if you don't, this is what you will hear: "I'm cold! I'm bloody cold!!! Can you not see this??? I have no bag!! I'm wearing the same clothes I've been wearing for thirty-six hours!!!! I don't know anyone!! And I'm *cooooooooold*!!!!!!!!!!!!!"

I'll never forget the look of shock on his face—his eyes got very wide, and his Dudley Do-Right jaw dropped. "Fuck!" he said (a man of many words), as though I had just asked for a twelve-course meal (that he would have to pay for). I jumped out of the car and began to roam the streets of Christchurch. See, this is always a good trick. Men don't want you roaming the streets; it sets off something primal in them, as if you may become mating prey for another beast. Besides, he was hell-bent on impressing me with his wonderful birthplace, since he felt it was akin to Bethlehem. He drove around and found me, I conceded to getting back in the car, my point was made, and we went to a store and bought a jacket. And you don't even want to know how I felt about not having my jammies. Hold on a sec, I'm shivering.

Which leads me to mention some interesting facts about me. I can travel without anything at all *except:* a high-thread-count cotton sheet, a fan, my medication (don't say it), and my pajamas. If I love you a lot, I'll sleep naked. That's it. Because anything else you can buy, but I need these things immediately; my peace of mind depends on them. When I went to the Tour de France, I didn't have the proper adapter to make my fan work, and I practically slept with the guy at the hotel who rewired it. I love coconut cream pie. I've never broken a bone. And I've never written a book. Maybe you can tell.

18
Bring a Sweater

These Four Walls, *2006*

Up on the rooftop I can remember
Borders I had to break.
Now I can see I had this life
To make.

My former manager told me once while I was out doing press and radio promotion all day and a show every night, "The show is the least important part of the day." I was shocked and offended to the core. He was implying that the promo push was the most crucial thing, but it isn't so. The most important thing, every day and every night, is what to wear. And that's how I began to write for my next record, *These Four Walls*. With an ode to a dress.

As usual I was low on material—I hadn't written anything since *Whole New You* bombed. While I was on tour during the summer of 2003, I was booked at Red Butte Garden in Salt Lake City. Things were finally coming back into balance after divorce número dos and the change-up in labels and managers. My new manager, Ken Levitan, got me off Columbia and onto Nonesuch, a small label under the umbrella of Warner Brothers. Emmylou Harris told me one time that she loved her record label. I'd never, ever heard anyone say that. She was on Nonesuch, and that's where I wanted to go. Ken managed a lot of my friends and colleagues and mentors: Emmylou, John Hiatt, Lyle Lovett, Patty Griffin, Buddy and Julie Miller. I was in good company.

My dressing room at the garden in Salt Lake that afternoon was an amazing greenhouse on a hill overlooking the basin, and I noticed that I was content. It was time to get ready for my show, so I put on a light, sheer, airy dress that I loved, by a company called Dosa. I felt satisfied, happy. It occurred to me to jot something down.

> *I put on my finest summer dress,*
> *So light and thin, it was my best.*
> *I brushed my hair, I held my breath,*
> *I went out to face the wilderness,*
> *I went out to face the wilderness.*

I liked it. That was the first thing I'd written in a really long time. You know, one of the major pleasures in my life is buying clothes. I get visceral, tactile, visual satisfaction out of clothing—the sculpture, the textures, the colors. It's an art form. It makes a big difference to me, the clothes I choose to put on my body. Which doesn't necessarily mean they have to be expensive or fancy, although that often helps. "Summer Dress" gives a more hopeful version of the character that I tend to write about, who feels oppressed by her surroundings. This time she gets free, but not without the proper wardrobe.

All the songs on *These Four Walls* were written primarily in a two- or three-week period during which I went to a studio in Austin called Cedar Creek. Technology being what it is, I had MP3s of tracks with the music John had written, which were downloaded to a software program called Nuendo. I could sit by myself at a computer, with a good microphone, press a button, and record melodies, nonsense, as many ideas as I could come up with, over these tracks. Bit by bit, they began to take shape.

Writing is like a sport. You have to show up, and you have to practice. Yes, there are times that are more or less convenient, and there are times when you are more or less motivated. But it's about showing up. Some days the lyrics just start to come out from an unconscious part of you. Other times you're so conscious of them not coming out that you want to scream. And sometimes you do. Scream. But as long as you keep making yourself available to the music and to the emotions you will fill it with, good things can happen. As I started the process this time, I was having some trouble making any good things happen. I was, as they say in the writing biz, totally blocked.

If writing is a sport, I was in desperate need of a coach. Stokes came to Austin to help, and he did this exercise with me where he would take little phrases out of the newspaper and make me write them down. Then he'd give me a certain amount of time to use them in a song. It's a great exercise, because it makes you realize that whatever you write, it's going to take you somewhere. "Fill Me Up" was one of the phrases he gave me, and that became the title for a great, uplifting piece of music I had from John. To me it's always been a song to my audience, and to Callie.

I wrote a line when I was at my sister's one day: "I'm gonna die in these four walls." I meant it from a humorous standpoint at that time. Kay lives in the suburbs of Austin. It was Sunday, and the kids were playing in the pool. The adults were outside, too, drinking beer and grilling burgers. There were sports inside on the TV. It was just the way I had grown up. And there we were again. I thought, *Whoa, I am really dug in.*

When I moved back to Austin in 1994, I always felt as if (and it sounds so morbid) this was a good place to die. There was just something about it for me. There always has been. So I took that one step further in "These Four Walls" and adopted the point of view of somebody who's nearing the end of her life, looking back—not with regret, just with appreciation and wistful sentiment, at peace. The guitar music by John is very simple to play, and it moved me immediately, so much so that I was hesitant to go after it, but I found the heart of it, I think.

Many years prior I had written the lines "Hey everybody in the old schoolyard, / We took it all the way and we took it hard," to an old musical idea of John's that I'd always liked. The phrase "tough kid" came to me, and the song, titled "Tuff Kid," followed pretty quickly. It's basically about me in junior high and high school, a kid having a hell of a time of it at home but armed, in this case, with her guitar, which was fast becoming her identity.

"Cinnamon Road" to me is mainly just imagery. John unknowingly inspired it. He told me one day about the place where he kept all the painful memories in his life; he said it was like they were in a box somewhere. It's about regret, it's about longing, it's about the past. It's the idea that no matter what you do, the things that anchor you and even the things that weigh you down are always going to be the same, your whole life. The events that devastate you, the lovers and friends and family you lose—the things that by all accounts you're supposed to get over, I guess, but I don't think you do. I don't think you ever do. I don't think it ever goes away.

"The Bird" was started from a scrap of paper that I had, scribbled with the words "What I like about the bird . . ." I call it my low-self-esteem song, and it's similar in theme to "Another Long One" from my first record. I did have a dream about an old boyfriend, which starts the song. I dreamed that we were young again, that I wasn't a needy, dysfunctional alcoholic and I knew how to be empathetic and giving.

I was going through a phase that's never really ended, I guess, where I was decorating my house. I want color, and I want clutter. Sparse does not work for me. It needs to be a little crazy. I really appreciate houses that have white walls and beautiful artwork and negative space, but I can't do it. For at least two years, maybe longer, I was putting samples of color on my wall—and that appears in "Fill Me Up" when I mention "French blue" and "the right shade of tangerine." I wouldn't doubt that I had a hundred quarts of paint in my garage and totally patchworked walls of this color, that color. It was insane.

One of the colors was named Venetian Blue. I thought it had a romantic ring to it, but I couldn't really get anywhere with it until I saw *Brokeback Mountain*. Something about the Heath Ledger character stayed with me for a long time. Just walking down the street, sitting at a desk, anything—I'd have that moment where I'd stop and say, "Who is it that I'm thinking about? It's someone I know." And it was Ennis Del Mar. I wrote "Venetian Blue" from Ennis's point of view, about being apart from the one you love and the anticipation of a time when you'll see that person again, and set it to this very languid piece of music John had written. I was able to use the melting of ice and snow as a metaphor for the melting of your heart that you've had to keep hard in order to survive until you're reunited.

Meanwhile, I had met someone new, and when I meet someone and I begin to fall in love, there's an essential discomfort for me, because I tend to lose myself. I have impulses and needs that I have to ignore, or quell, because they're not appropriate, such as wanting to pick out the wedding china after the first introduction.

Several months into our courtship I wrote "I'm Gone" while I was at a hotel in Philadelphia and couldn't fall asleep. I found myself obsessing over this new man in my life. Surprise! As I lay in bed, my anxieties were swirling around, and I began to worry that I was in over my head. I really liked this guy, and I wanted it to work. And this desperation set in—which I hate. I was pretty pissed off to be going through that; I was sick of it, like I was always going to be on the same treadmill when it came to falling in love. It's a typical chain reaction for me: fall in love, feel absolute terror, which manifests itself as massive insecurity, which spells doom. I wrote the line "Over and over and over and over." I wanted to be relaxed and sleepy and simply pleased about the process of getting to know someone, but all I was was tormented about wanting love from a man, from an audience, from the record company, from critics. In moments like that, because your pride and attempts at control and civility break down, you just let yourself go. You don't care about being seen as desperate for approval. I wrote, "There are things I will do for a hatchet job, too," and it felt good. I was so angry. How far would I go, how deeply would I betray myself to be loved? At the end of each chorus is the wish to be able to just walk away. *I'm gone.* I get a lot of satisfaction out of singing that song. It's a bitter song, and I enjoy the bitterness of it. The music is a pretty simple chord progression that I put down in Garage Band one day.

Would a country artist please cut "Let It Slide"? I wrote the first part of that song ages ago, and then John and I wrote the chorus for it much later on. It's an example of a good, lighthearted, semi-pop song. Could it have been successful in another time and place? I got to sing it with Teddy Thompson—I love his voice.

I had to convince John about "So Good to See You." I'd started it several years earlier. To me the interesting part of the song, the reason I continued to be motivated to try to write it, lay in wanting to come up with a piece where the singer has her defenses up. She's trying to express herself with a lot of fancy rhetoric—ordinarily, intermittently, essentially, pointedly—a literary pompousness that's basically saying, "When you cut away the bullshit, I'm still in love with you." Then she just comes right out with it in the chorus.

John had this bizarre chaise lounge in his studio, a lawn chair. I guess he would take a nap in it sometimes, I don't know. And he had come up with a very lush piece of music that I wanted to put lyrics to. He said, "Well, to loosen you up on this song, just lie here and I'll hand you a microphone, and let's see what happens."

Two things came out. I had seen a PBS special on Martin Luther King Jr. the night before. There were clips of many of his great speeches, and that's where "That Don't Worry Me Now" came from. That's not what he said. He said, "I'm not worried about anything," and I paraphrased. The other thing that turned up was the biblical story of Jacob wrestling with the angel, and this was on my mind because I was obsessed with the HBO production of *Angels in America,* where the story of Jacob is key. I know how I feel when I sing it. I know it resonates and brings satisfaction to me to say that the angels are boring. I know it's not true that these things don't worry me—they do. I just like the beauty of the tune paired up with a sort of agnostic sentiment;

there's an odd kind of hope in that song, something about the simple basic premise of living and dying that we all share.

As we were mixing *These Four Walls,* we would sometimes go out of the control room and into the studio, and John would play the piano or he'd play the guitar or bass. He's one of those guys who can't be without an instrument in his hands. He'd start a song that we both knew—a Beatles song, or a Beach Boys song, and sometimes I would start singing along. We were just goofing off. And one of the songs that he played ended up being "Words," by the Bee Gees. I've always loved that song. I looked up the lyrics on the Internet, and in five minutes I'd figured out how to play it. We pressed the RECORD button, I played the guitar and sang, and John played the bass. And that was that. As someone who writes lyrics and finds a lot of joy and satisfaction in singing not only my own lyrics but lyrics that I think are great by other people, I thought there was something poignant about the line "It's only words, and words are all I have to take your heart away."

We recorded *These Four Walls* at New York Noise on Gansevoort Street in the Meatpacking District during the winter of 2005 and 2006. To support the record in that spring, I had an idea for a touring trio that would include Buddy Miller, my old bandmate, and Deborah Dobkin, a great percussionist. Lo and behold, they were both available and interested. When we played Town Hall in New York, both Larry Campbell and John Leventhal sat in. The circle had come around. We were all still playing and doing well. It was such a moment of pride and satisfaction.

I had a new record, a new tour, a new band, and a new guy. And "I'm Gone" was going to prove to be more prophetic than I could have realized.

19

I'm Hypnotized

**Over and over and over and over,
I'm beckoning, begging, I keep hanging on.**

"All done, heading west." It was right there on his computer screen, the e-mail from my ex-boyfriend to his new girlfriend. I knew what he was all done with—he had come back to Austin to move out of the apartment he'd rented here to be closer to me. I knew he was back because he'd asked me to have coffee with him. I looked at his e-mail because after having coffee, even after sleeping together, after he told me he loved me, he was still leaving. He wished me good luck—good luck!—and drove away. It was a gorgeous spring day in March. The trees had budded, and the bluebonnets and Indian paintbrushes were blooming. He hated Austin.

After my second divorce, I thought if I ever coupled again, I would end up with a balding, boring man with a belly and ugly shoes, someone who did executive marketing, but no, this one had surfer hair and great teeth. He was a big, silly, goofball, knucklehead boy-man, with money. His clothes were scruffily perfect. The sweetness, and how much we laughed, how hard we laughed. Such a funny man, such a charming man, such a luggy, adorable teddy-bear man. The only criterion I had for my next boyfriend was that he be employed, but this—oh, my Lord. And he liked to shop—that alone was reason enough for me to want to marry him.

Once when we were in New York, we went to the G-Star Raw store and he bought some camo pants. After we got back to the hotel, I said, "Come try on your stuff." He stripped down, put on the pants, jumped on top of the bed, and launched into a Maori war dance, right there on the bed, crouching and slapping his thighs and sticking out his tongue and yelling. Apparently this was either a rugby psych-out or a New Zealand mating ritual, but I found myself staring openmouthed at this spectacle and thinking, *Oh, my god, I'm falling in love with this guy.* What does this tell you?

And similarly, I had done something when we first met that bewitched him. A group of us went somewhere for ice cream after dinner, and the subject of *The Andy Griffith Show* came up. I'm something of a trivia buff when it comes to Andy Griffith, and it turned out he had been watching it a lot with his kids. I asked if he happened to notice that in some episodes Floyd the barber is standing up but in some he stays seated and never stands up. This, I went on, was because the actor had had a stroke and was unable to stand, so he was filmed always sitting. To further my point, given that *I* was sitting, I did a little imitation of Floyd. "Ooooh, Andy!" was the extent of it, but that's all it took—he fell in love with me. So we have the Maori dancer and Floyd the barber, and that was the basis of our attraction.

It was the spring of 2006, and I was doing really well, due in no small part to the fact that I was almost done with *These Four Walls.* Writing songs is hard work for me, and I am always truly amazed when I finally have a collection of them fit for release. The dust had settled between Mario and me; we were coparenting amicably, and Callie was thriving. I wasn't dating much and wasn't particularly lonely. The antidepressant meds I was on seemed to be holding. In short, I felt solid, productive. I was ready to fall in love again.

We went to dinner. He held my hand. I went home to Austin. He called constantly, sent flowers, jewelry, cards, and all sorts of silly trinkets, like the plastic nun toy that slaps a ruler and shoots sparks from her mouth when you wind her up. FedEx boxes came with Charleston Chews, seashells, lava rocks, dental floss, earrings. There was one bracelet in particular, a sleek silver modern sort of piece that I adored. (His children, upon seeing it, exclaimed, "Mummy has one just like it! In gold!")

He wasn't divorced yet, but that didn't stop him from asking me if I would think about getting married again. In an effort to understand it all much later, I consulted a number of self-help books that helped me realize I'd been a victim of "blowtorching," a term used for the full-court press of the come-on, the chase times a million, usually going in short order from hot pursuit to cold feet and ending in disaster. I had been divorced from my daughter's father for six years. I had gone on maybe four dates since then. I raised Callie, and I traveled for work. In other words, I was ripe for the picking; I was fresh meat for a blowtorcher.

I had never heeded anyone's advice in matters of the heart. ("It takes time to get to know someone!" "He's only separated, not divorced!") No, true love made all things possible. This was it. I had our lives planned out within three months of our first date. My daughter and I would spend time with him in the summer while I toured. He would come to Austin. We would travel back and forth. It would be easy. Nothing to it. We both had freedom and enough money. It was exciting, and it was meant to be. This was the next chapter of my life. I wasn't going to have to raise my child alone, wasn't going to have to grow old alone.

In reality I hung on for a couple of years, sometimes happily, mostly not, while he backpedaled at breakneck pace and I pretended not to notice. Then he decided to move to Hawaii and didn't seem the least bit concerned that this was long distance and a half. When I asked how we would see each other, he would kind of shrug and say he would have to come to the mainland to see his kids at some point. Not encouraging. There were tears in hotels, tears backstage, tears in planes, trains, and automobiles.

He officially called it quits, although I was the one who asked if he thought we should break up. Don't you hate that, when they leave you no choice but to acknowledge the misery? And it somehow looks like your idea? I describe it as having a gun put to your head, only it's you who has to pull the trigger. I asked why now? He said he couldn't navigate all this. And then the crusher: "I love you, Shawn, but I don't love you enough to stay in Austin." Except I never asked him to be in Austin. He hated Austin.

"Your relationship is a scab!" That's what Billy said to me. Billy was this last boyfriend's best friend. He had become my sounding board since the breakup. For one thing, Stokes, my usual expert on a man's perspective, had gone AWOL. Stokes had fallen in love and, like me, tends to see no gray area between ecstasy and hell when it comes to these matters. I could rarely track him down—he was at the stage where the two of them were oblivious to other life-forms.

So I turned to Billy. Only a numbskull confides in the ex's best friend while in the throes of rejection, but this was as close to talking to the ex as I could get. Billy was something of a legend when it came to how many women from Match.com a man in his fifties could bed in quick succession.

Billy didn't seem to mind talking to me. He had a lot to say about relationships in general. But about the ex he would only offer, "Maybe he'll miss you . . . *and maybe he won't.*" He asked me what was I going to do about finding a new boyfriend. He told me that if he lived in Austin, he would date me. He said he had to be careful or he might develop a crush on me. And still I did not see it coming. I was as libidinous as a cow patty. So one horrible day, as I was blathering on to Billy, he abruptly asked me where I was. I was in my room. Then he whispered, "Are you lying down?" Oh. Oh, swell. My confidant is trying to have phone sex with me as I'm crying real live tears over his best friend. I made light of it, but I felt as though a drooling pervert had just thrust his hand down my pants. The last thing I needed was to be naked and vulnerable with the gigolo of Match.com for Seniors, who gave not a rusty fuck what kind of condition I was in. There are places to go for things like that, and they make Match.com look like a glass of lemonade on the front porch.

DOM was my name for the ex, or one of them anyway. He liked to be teased and made fun of—it was his way of apologizing for or admitting to bad behavior while simultaneously getting off the hook, the old self-deprecation trick. One night—in fact, it may have been the night of the breakup sex after he'd moved out of his apartment in Austin—when he was still pondering and waffling about whether he was an ocean person or a mountain person, being sick to death of the subject, I feigned mock exasperation (no, you read that double negative correctly—the exasperation was real): "Would you stop it already, you dumb old man??"

This delighted him. He laughed and laughed. I abbreviated "dumb old man" to DOM. He liked it. He'd been searching for the proper way to identify himself in regard to me since the breakup. Something personal yet not intimate. He had similar trouble when we first fell in love and he was introducing me as his "friend." I finally said, "Could you at least introduce me as the friend who sucks your cock?"

I did hear from him again, though, several months after our breakup. By way of snail mail, I got a congratulatory card for my Grammy nomination in 2010. And I got a "happy birthday" text the next month. Signed "DOM." I threw away the card and deleted the text, and I was okay. I was okay.

When I first met him, he recited a long list of his wife's accusations against him. She said he was manipulative, cold, chameleon-like, emotionally unavailable, passive-aggressive, and greedy. *Oh, my God, she's a nutcase,* I thought. Because this guy is as innocent as a lamb. "He's an open book," claimed the man who introduced us. "I'm an open book!" he cried in his own defense more than once.

The Open Book became harder to crack than the da Vinci Code. The Open Book is in another language. The Open Book is dedicated to no one. The Open Book has some pages missing. They will be the ones you need the most. You can study the Open Book as often as you like. There are quizzes. They make no sense. You resort to cheating to get the answers right. You make things up.

You open the book again and again, always hopeful. It's so glossy and beautiful. It smells like Fresh Sake Hair Cream. But it's blank, each page empty. This is what's really inside. Nothing.

20
Out of My Mind

1996

All through the night I can pretend
The morning will make me whole again.
And every day I can begin
To wait for the night again.

I guess I knew it was bad before I really said anything to the doctor. It had happened before, feeling bad but not wanting to admit it. I wanted it not to be true. When you're depressed, you don't feel like bothering about anything anyway—brushing your teeth and bathing are monumental tasks—and you have no perspective with which to gauge the worsening of your condition. You learn to look at the usual benchmarks: how you eat and sleep, if you're caring about your hygiene, if anything interests you besides sitting in a corner, and how elaborate or specific your suicidal thoughts are. And then there is the loathsome necessity of calling the doctor. Again.

The Prozac I'd been taking for eighteen years was no longer working, and my new doctor put me on Cymbalta. I gave it the requisite three weeks allotted for the drug to take effect, but nothing remarkable happened. So she, the doctor, raised the dosage. I waited again, this time longer, and still I was flat and disconnected and anxious and paralyzed. I went to see her again, ready to admit I wasn't getting better, as though it were my fault. That's what depressed people do. They think everything is their fault, especially the depression. Unfortunately, a lot of psychopharmacologists, like many doctors, are egomaniacs with lousy bedside manners, and inevitably I would reach a point of diminishing returns with them, either because they ran out of ideas or said something stupid. This doctor fell into both categories. I went in, lower than whale shit, with the disappointing news. I went in because I had to believe there was something else we could try and I needed her expertise to guide me there. The Cymbalta wasn't working, I told her. We needed a new strategy.

She looked at me, cocked her head to one side, and said brightly, "You know what I want you to do?" She said, "I want you to go home and watch comedies. I want you to find something, maybe on YouTube, that really, really cracks you up."

Are you kidding me? How do I explain what a ludicrous suggestion this is? We're talking clinical depression here, clinical depression that I'd been diagnosed with and treated for since I was nineteen years old. It's an illness. And her best idea was to try to make me laugh? That's like suggesting a Band-Aid for a long, deep gash. No, it's worse than that. It's like asking a blind person to see. I paid the $175 fee for that gem of a suggestion and stumbled out the door. Another one bites the dust. She basically told me to snap out of it, by far the *dumbest* thing you can say to somebody who's depressed.

I got in touch with a big-shot doctor in New York. He thought since Elavil had worked for me when I was nineteen, we should try it again. But first I had to quit the Cymbalta, and he said— and I quote—"Cymbalta is a bitch to get off of." To get off Cymbalta as safely as possible, I had to start taking . . . Prozac.

This would put us at about March of 2009. My relationship ended in January 2008, over a year prior. It was impossible to tell at this point where the emotional fallout from that ended and the clinical depression began. I had certainly been depressed before and had been dumped before, too, but this time the convergence of chemistry and situation made for a sort of sinister alchemy. I can say with certainty that I'd been sliding downhill since even before the breakup. I was jumpy and massively oversensitive. I cried because I didn't have the right jacket. I cried because we were driving on a curvy road. I cried because of the way the sun was shining. I cried because a car honked its horn. I was crying because I was depressed.

Then the breakup. I admitted myself to a psychiatric facility in Austin at some point in the spring of 2008, because I was unable to do anything but cry. I stayed for a few hours, until I realized I was more comfortable crying at home. I got in a long nap, had some bad food, and called my mother for a ride. Oh, well. I'd always wanted to know what the nuthouse was like, just in case. Now I knew. I fired the comedy doctor, and the big-shot New York doctor came into play. It was during a music cruise, in February 2009, that I started the process of getting off Cymbalta. I had begun the taper two days before the cruise, and by the second day on the boat I was basically not functioning. I would wake up, if I slept, to a depression so profound and paralyzing and frightening that it required two or three milligrams of Ativan to deliver relief by knocking me out. By evening I was able to do a show. I don't remember the shows, but I've been told I was not up to par, which hardly surprises me. I remember sinking into blackness within two hours of waking, crying uncontrollably, taking the Ativan, and shuffling around the deck until I knew I could sleep. Then I'd stay in bed until it got dark.

When we reached dry land after a week, I consulted the big shot. He added nortriptyline. I started having massive anxiety attacks. He concluded I was in a "mixed state," meaning a state of mania and depression concurrently. He scrapped the nortriptyline and added Depakote to control the mania. No change. A month went by, in which I did nothing but cry. The month of March 2009. Of course I thought of suicide, but I couldn't do that to my daughter.

My mother helped me in countless ways during all this, mostly to pinch-hit for me with Callie, getting her fed, entertaining her. I called her in the middle of the night on many, many occasions in the midst of an anxiety attack, and she would get up and drive to my house to be with me just as many times. I believe she would have done anything in her power to help me.

I got another doctor, this time in Austin. Dr. Lynn Spillar. She took me off Depakote, raised the Prozac dosage, reintroduced Abilify, and had me take Lunesta to get my sleep pattern back to normal. Very slowly I noticed I wasn't crying all the time and that I could function, however minimally, but I never fully recovered;

there was a piece of me missing. I *could* function, but only at the most base level. I was flat and disconnected and anxious and full of dread, scared to drive, scared to fly, scared to perform, scared to leave the house. This is when, at Dr. Spillar's suggestion, I called Sheppard Pratt, a psychiatric inpatient facility in Baltimore, to see if they had a bed for me. She also asked me to make an appointment with a doctor in Austin who administered ECT, electroconvulsive therapy. The meds weren't cutting it, that was that. Time for the big guns.

Dr. Spillar had one more idea before we tried ECT, and I thought it was a terrible one. She wanted me to try a stimulant. I'd all my life had panic attacks, and even a cup of coffee could put me over the edge. I was a drunk; I liked downers. A stimulant seemed counterintuitive, but I was at the point where I certainly had nothing to lose. It was November 9, 2009. Callie was scheduled to spend the weekend with her father, and I knew I couldn't stand being in my house alone for three days. I got online and booked a Southwest flight to Providence, Rhode Island, by way of Baltimore, to see Carolyn.

Carolyn Rosenfeld is my guardian angel. Look up "selfless" in the dictionary, you will find her name. When we met eighteen years ago, she handled corporate accounts for a graphics company in Providence, but, loving music as she does, she also did favors here and there for a great club called Lupo's Heartbreak Hotel—things like picking up artists from the airport. That's how I met her. Bit by bit over the years, I've worn her down and now she works for me for a tenth of what she used to make, and for twice the effort. Carolyn travels with me. Carolyn was on the boat trip. She walked me around the deck, put me to bed, got me up. Carolyn is my friend. She is my child's godmother. It was Carolyn who stayed with me in Austin for an entire month while I was having what can only be called a nervous breakdown.

Me and Carolyn Rosenfeld, 2010

I filled the script for the stimulant Concerta, normally used as an ADD drug. I threw it in my bag, determined to try it, but only once I was with Carolyn, so she could talk me down when I started to trip on this shit. I got to the airport in Austin, and it was the oddest thing—I boarded the plane, and there in an aisle seat was Dr. Lynn Spillar. She was attending a conference in Baltimore. I took the window seat beside her. I have to say this is one of the times in my life where I believe absolutely that I was witnessing a higher power in action. Truly, it was in my face, it was a sign. I couldn't have felt safer if it had been Mother Teresa in that aisle seat. We didn't talk much, but it didn't matter. I got to Providence. It was Friday. I got up Saturday morning, took that damn pill, and set out for the mall. When in doubt, shop, that is my motto.

I felt better inside of two hours.

I felt better. Something clicked. I had that elusive, intangible something back—I felt like me. I could relax, I could laugh, I could think. I wasn't just waiting to die anymore. There was the possibility of life being *positive*. The ex receded in my mind, became abstract, a phantom insect I could swat away. I wanted to cook dinner, I wanted to have conversations, I wanted to hear music. I swear, it was a miracle. I was *back*. Dr. Spillar was on the same plane home to Austin from Baltimore on Sunday. I told her what had happened. "You needed dopamine," she said. Dopamine regulates one's sense of pleasure. Jesus H. God.

I looked over my shoulder for months, but it held, this cocktail of Prozac, Abilify, and Concerta. I told Spillar that the stimulant was the magic bullet. She stood up for the other two drugs, saying that for whatever reason there was a harmonic convergence among all three. While all of them may have played a part in leveling my depression, Concerta was the superhero that kicked its ass and took its name.

21
Her Favorite Room

Me and Callie at the Grammys, 2010

Singing back home to you,
Laughing back home to you,
Dragging back home to you.

I have two homes. One is in Austin, Texas. It's eclectically chaotic. It's colorful. The living-room walls are Brigade (a deep marine blue), the kitchen cabinets are Fig (chartreuse), the office is Flower Pot. For my bedroom I went with wallpaper called Chiang Mai Dragon by Schumacher in the mocha colorway. Very strong choice. I live with my daughter. This summer, at the age of twelve, Callie decided not to go on the road with me for the first time. She's starting to make her own life, just as I did. I still talk to my friends from junior high school—Janey, Liz, Mandy, Joanne, and Todd. That's what I wish for Callie, that she'll have the kind of friends I do. She picked out the color for her own room. It's Venetian Blue.

My other home is with all of you.

Whether it's been in vans or buses, or limos or airplanes, I've spent much of the last thirty-five years on tour. It's been my privilege to be wanted and to give what I truly love to give for all this time. I always wanted to play music, my whole life. My audience allows me to, and it's an honor. I've played festivals, amphitheaters, state fairs, countless clubs and theaters in every single state in the Union (including Alaska and Hawaii). I've played the Dead Sea, Europe, China, Australia, and New Zealand. Even Carnegie Hall.

And over the years I've been lucky enough to get the opportunity to meet and sometimes to perform with many of my heroes and colleagues. Now, bear with me. It's a long list. But this South Dakota geek of a girl still cannot believe it. So here goes: Sting, Lyle Lovett, Jackson Browne, John Hiatt, Bruce Hornsby, Bonnie Raitt, David Crosby, Graham Nash, Neil Young, Paul Simon, James Taylor, Joni Mitchell, Jane Siberry, Victoria Williams, Elton John, Bernie Taupin, Paul McCartney, Neil Finn, the Band, Chris Whitley, Jesse Winchester, Chris Hillman, Stephen Stills, Odetta, Judy Collins, Rosanne Cash, Rodney Crowell,

Bob Dylan, Elvis Costello, Chrissie Hynde, Roger Daltrey, Patti Smith, Bruce Springsteen, Carole King, the Eagles, Ringo, Eric Idle, Stevie Nicks, Sheryl Crow, David Gray, Chris Isaak, Richard Thompson, Loudon Wainwright, Emmylou Harris, Patty Griffin, Alison Krauss, Mary Chapin Carpenter, Dar Williams, the Cowboy Junkies, the Indigo Girls, Tony Bennett, Neil Finn, Sarah McLachlan, Brandi Carlile, Steve Earle, Paula Cole, Jason Mraz—even 'N Sync, Bill Clinton, Ernie from *Sesame Street,* and Spinal Tap. Blessed!

"The Sensitive Ones"—Jackson Browne, Shawn Colvin, Bonnie Raitt, and Bruce Hornsby—on The Tonight Show *with Jay Leno, 1999* (Paul Drinkwater/ NBCU Photo Bank via AP Images)

Me with Jackson and Lyle, 1990

Me with Mary Chapin Carpenter and Rosanne Cash at Bob Fest, 1992

Me and Neil Finn, London, 1992

Me and Socks, the White House cat, 1993

Me with Sheryl Crow and Bob Dylan, Grammys, 1998

Me and Mary Chapin Carpenter, Philly Folk Fest, 1988

The road can be a fickle mistress. It runs from the sublime to the surreal. Take, for example, a gig I once did in Seattle. Or, more specifically, Federal Way, Washington. I ended up in Federal Way because I was the prize in a Gallo Wine sweepstakes. The people from Gallo approached me and asked if I would be willing to be the featured artist in a sweepstakes they would promote for the summer of 2001. At the end of the summer, the winner would be chosen, I would travel to the winner's home for a private concert, and for this I would be paid. A lot. *Well, hell, nobody loses,* I thought. One of my ardent fans would be rewarded with my presence, and I would get some cash, and all for simply being the poster child for Gallo Wine for a summer. And so I said, "Of course."

It's helpful to know a couple of things up front here: One, ask yourself who enters a sweepstakes? Do you? I don't. Two, I don't always travel well. The panic is most likely to set in on the road when I'm alone and disconnected, and I never know when this is more or less likely to occur—it's a crapshoot. For this reason I always have a little pill with me called Ativan. It's the same tranquilizer that Steuart Smith used in his planephobia cocktail. Now, let's assume it doesn't help matters if I go to Seattle and immediately have a gigantic mocha latte, just because I'm in Seattle, home of Starbucks. So here I am, alone in Seattle and tanked up on caffeine, which for me is basically an anxiety attack in a cup.

I realize I'm about to go to a stranger's home to perform. Up until that point, I'd made an assumption that whoever won the sweepstakes would want the prize. But when the Gallo people picked me up to take me to Federal Way, they looked sheepish and I sensed trouble. I got in the backseat of the car, shut the door, and began to think twice.

Who were the winners? I asked. Nice people. Did they know me? Sort of. Was it a nice house? Well, there were dogs. Oh, Lord.

What had I done? My fantasy was that the winners would be overwhelmed at the prospect of having me in their home. Their home, of course, would be perched on a cliff somewhere, and the throng that gathered would sip pinot and query me on the meaning of my work. Now I was forced to consider otherwise.

I got that horrible, trapped feeling, like when your parents took you to see your weird cousins and you had no choice but to live in their funny-smelling house with the wrong food and the wrong pets and having to hear that prayer every night about dying before you wake. Well, I seized up. I was in a vehicle driven by strangers bound for the great unknown, and I suddenly had terrible misgivings and no time to consider them and no choice to change things even if I wanted to. My heart raced, my hands began to sweat, my head spun, and I couldn't breathe. "Pull over," I said.

I got out of the car at a strip mall and called a friend to shore me up. "I'm having an anxiety attack, and my head is leaving my body." The thing about panic attacks is that in that moment you truly feel that what's happening is a matter of life and death, that you may have a heart attack or go insane or disintegrate or do all three at the same time. My friend told me to take an Ativan. "But I have to play," I said. "If your head is leaving your body, I suggest you take a pill." She had a point. Understand, though, that I had not nipped this episode in the bud when I felt it coming on and was now in a full-fledged, paralyzing, peaking panic attack. That one pitiful little tiny white pill seemed rather impotent, given the circumstances. So I took two.

The folks in Federal Way were down-to-earth, lovely people with several Barcaloungers, and they had no idea who I was. The house was filled with doilies and ceramic frogs and Hummel figurines. I felt no pain when I finally got there to grace them with my presence. I said, "It's your party, what do you want to hear?" A nice man mentioned that some Merle Haggard would be nice. So I played some Merle, exceedingly grateful to Buddy Miller at that moment. Next came a request for "Johnny" Denver. I stipulated that this was to be a sing-along, and when the chorus for "Take Me Home, Country Roads" came around, the Barcaloungers flew back in ecstasy and everyone joined in. And so it went. I don't remember the drive back to Seattle, I don't remember getting to the hotel, I don't even remember going home the next day. The lesson learned here is this: Some of us don't enter sweepstakes because we take them for a scam. I'm here to tell you, it's not true.

Not long after Callie was born, I was invited to be part of a show in Orlando, Florida, at Disney World—thanks to the success of "Sunny Came Home"—for a Christmas special they were taping. One of the other acts was 'N Sync. I remember being at a press conference with Justin Timberlake—he must have been about twelve—and I'm pretty sure Joey Fatone was making eyes at me. We all did a finale together of a bouncy Donny Hathaway song called "This Christmas." I wasn't playing guitar—we had a great band, and acoustic guitar wasn't necessary. I think I may have made mention earlier of the fact that I'm not particularly coordinated. This is another reason I play the guitar. During a ballad I can manage having nothing to do with my hands if I have to, but if the song is cooking along, I can't resist dancing. And the finale song was a great, up-tempo, R&B-flavored tune. So here I was with this teenage-boy band, and they were kicking it. I couldn't help it, I jumped up and down a couple of times—and from having just had a baby my pelvic floor got stretched out or something. I peed in my panty hose when I jumped during that song, which gave me the perspective in a very brutal way that I was a lot older than the boys in 'N Sync. I looked over at Joey, but he was done with me, off in another world. Now I keep my guitar onstage in my arms and my moves where they belong—at home.

Then there was the one and only time I played in Columbia, Missouri. It was summer, and the gig was outdoors—that's all I knew. I don't need much information about where or when I'm playing, as long as somebody can point me in the right direction at the right time. As I was being driven to the site, though, I noticed something rather strange: There was a large marquee bordering the grounds that read FAIR. Usually in the summer I play festivals or city concerts in the park. I barely had a chance to consider what "fair" might mean when I read the rest of the marquee. Next, in gigantic letters, was:

TRACTOR PULL
and underneath *that*—
Shawn Colvin

Ruh-roh. Suddenly I was wide awake. Something told me I wasn't in Kansas anymore, but strangely enough that's almost exactly where I was. I wasn't far from Kansas, and Kansas wasn't far from South Dakota, so these would be "my people," wouldn't they? I looked around, and I wasn't so sure. I saw fencing—stalls. I knew what that meant, but I asked anyway. "Are there cows in there?" My driver answered, "Yes, ma'am, this is an agricultural show! That's where we keep the livestock!" He turned to give me a dazzling, friendly smile. "And," he continued, "the people who pay to see the cows get to see you for *free!*"

I sat bolt upright. I had my work cut out for me. The tractor-pull site and the concert grounds were one and the same. Fortunately, the tractor pull wasn't until the following night. I said a silent prayer of thanks for my days with the Dixie Diesels and the Buddy Miller Band. I had a feeling that some Merle Haggard was going to come in handy once again. I sat backstage, across from a shack where one could see a calf get born—*all day*—and brushed up on my country chops. But when I went to face the music, literally, I couldn't have been more surprised. There were people in Columbia, Missouri, who had braved the livestock show just to come see *me*. Hell, they might even have paid to see the cows without knowing it. I've seen this again and again—some of the gigs that I'd swear were going to be duds have turned out great.

Like the first time I played Salt Lake City. I mean, I just assumed that the whole town was Mormon and that either they'd not come at all or they'd be really subdued. No. Those people were *nuts*. I had a gig in Copper Mountain, Colorado, just a few weeks ago that was set up in a tent at the bottom of the mountain. The tent was cavernous. It was a free show for people who had done a long hike that day to raise money for MS. I assumed that no one would listen, because all of them would be (a) tired, and/or (b) interested in only the free food and drink. Also that the sound would be crummy. Wrong. They were perfect, and the sound was lovely. In Paris a few years ago, I played in a tiny church where I drew two hundred people. I had my guard up for that one, too. But you've never seen so many nice French people together in one place. And they were *fans*. Calling out for even my lesser-known numbers: " 'Tuff Keed'! 'Tuff Keed'! "

There was a time when I would go on tour all alone. It started when I was with Simon. If he was working with Richard, I'd just go out by myself. There was something about knowing that somewhere someone who loved me was keeping track of my comings and goings, and even in a state of constant motion I felt grounded. Then I married Mario and had Callie, and for the first four years of her life the two of them traveled with me much of the time. After Callie started school, I cut my touring back as much as possible for the school year and took her with me during the big summer tours. But around 2004 I hit a wall.

I was having a really bad day. I was in Minneapolis and wanted to quit my job. Being on the road was really taxing me; I felt trapped and burned out, exhausted, used up. I had to go and play outdoors at the Minnesota State Fair, a place where you can get anything you want fried on a stick. At outdoor gigs there were usually dogs, kids, hula hoops, hacky sacks, and without a doubt beer, beer, and more beer. I made calls to friends to center myself, I cried, I smoked, I ruminated. I felt angry at everything and at no one in particular. What in the name of God was I doing at the Minnesota State Fair? Who did they think I was—Garrison Keillor? No, it was just me, doing my job. I walked out onstage to do my set, prepared for the worst—a flat performance, a noisy audience. And then this thing happened:

It was like the channels of purity and musicality and dynamics just completely opened up. It had something to do with being bled out. This has happened to me before when I've been very broken down. It's as though there's some kind of artifice that comes along with coping well—one has to have some defenses up in order to function—and it's as though this artifice collapses temporarily.

When I have a performance like that, it's as if I can't miss. The playing—it's a miraculous, effortless thing. My fingers just seem to float and glide on the strings. It's like having sex with the instrument, and it's good sex. The coupling is perfect, the timing is perfect, the instrument is speaking to me and answering me, and I'm having a deep, connected, meaningful moment linking my voice and my words and my instrument. And emotionally charged—in an effortless way. Then the audience comes into play, and we're all part of this incredibly intimate experience. They become just as important an element, because I feel that they're feeling what I am. That's what happened at the Minnesota State Fair that afternoon.

For twelve years I've toured with my daughter, in some way, shape, or form every year. We've been on countless tour buses and visited too many zoos to name. I nursed her before and after shows, slept with her in a one-person bunk on the bus, swam with her in Bora-Bora, looked for Madeline in Paris but found her in London in Hyde Park with Miss Clavel and Pepito (for the uninitiated, Madeline is a little girl in a series of books by Ludwig Bemelmans). We have had several nannies: Monique turned Callie on to Queen and Hüsker Dü; Cynthia saw us through the divorce. On the road Callie made scrapbooks and videos with Jessica, and Vanessa taught her to straighten her hair and use makeup. We know every inch of Disneyland and the shortest route to the Central Park carousel, which she referred to as "sail ponies." Most of all, being a working mother, I have missed her when I've had to be away.

She calls. She's sick. I'm on the road. It's not serious, just a slight fever and a sore throat and a cough, but enough to keep her home from school. The nanny or my mother will have to take care of her, because her father has to go to work. She'll need to be taken to the doctor for a throat culture, because she always gets strep. I'm not there. I hated being sick as a kid and I needed my mother. I'm not there. She needs me. I'm at work, but I don't come home at five; I won't be home for another two weeks. She's sick. There's nothing I can do.

I'm not always performing by myself anymore. Recently I've had the pleasure of being part of a group again, Three Girls and Their Buddy, along with my friends Patty Griffin, Emmylou Harris, and my dear old bandmate Buddy Miller. As the years go by, I find that I treasure company on the road more than ever, and the musical brilliance of my cohorts here is off the charts.

Me with Patty Griffin, Buddy Miller, and Emmylou Harris—
Three Girls and Their Buddy—2008

Music heals me, answers my questions, soothes my agony, fires my ambition, creates and intensifies my joy. I was born loving music and, I believe, born to be a conduit for it. It is as though I always could and still can find an emotional solution or a reprieve or a response from learning and singing songs. Shortly after 9/11, I was asked to be part of a television special honoring the songs of Broadway, and I knew I had to try to sing something that spoke to the tragedy. I found it in one of my parents' old sound tracks that I grew up listening to, a song called "Try to Remember" from *The Fantasticks:*

> *Try to remember the kind of September*
> *When life was slow and oh, so mellow.*

Try to remember the kind of September
When grass was green and grain was yellow.
Try to remember the kind of September
When you were a tender and callow fellow.
Try to remember, and if you remember
Then follow.

Hearing my own singing and playing coming back to me still grounds me more than anything else. It doesn't matter if I'm in front of five people or five thousand. When I sing and play, I'm home.

Home

Epilogue

On a final note, let me mention again that always, whether times are good or bad or happy or sad, the most important thing is what I wore.

Age birth to sixth grade—Clothes my mother sewed. Red corduroy jumpers, et cetera.

Age seventh grade to college—Clothes I sewed. Peasant skirts, et cetera.

Carnegie Hall—I honestly don't remember when it was or who was there, but I wore Comme des Garçons from the fall/winter velvet and boiled-wool collection.

Steady On photo shoot—Old orange flight suit bought from Banana Republic when they still sold things like that. Jeans.

Fat City photo shoot—Jean Paul Gaultier, Frye boots.

Cover Girl photo shoot—Comme des Garçons.

A Few Small Repairs photo shoot—Nothing in particular and everything in between, and it doesn't matter anyway, because there's a painting on the cover.

Whole New You photo shoot—Papier-mâché mouse ears that no one found funny except me.

First Grammy Awards—Pleated black skirt, Thierry Mugler

chiffon shirt, Stephane Kélian boots. My friend Ellen called them "the boot of the season."

Big-win Grammy Awards—Jean Paul Gaultier dress, Ann Demeulemeester shoes.

Last Grammy Awards—Zac Posen dress, YSL necklace, Ann Demeulemeester boots.

Oprah—Marni jacket, jeans.

Johnny Carson—Vivienne Westwood.

Meeting James Taylor—Vintage fifties silk dress.

Meeting Joni Mitchell—Betsey Johnson caramel polka-dot silk slip dress.

Meeting Bill Clinton—Comme des Garçons, plaid boiled-wool men's shirt, Kangol hat, engineer boots.

First wedding—Lo New York crocheted dress.

Second wedding—Oh, my God, I have no idea.

Giving birth—Pratesi robe and a pair of my sister's socks.

Entire last year of my second marriage—CP Shades (i.e., fat and frumpy).

First date with ex—White long-sleeved waffle shirt, Girbaud black pants, dog-tag necklaces.

Morning of dumping—Muslin nightshirt from Mexico, egg on face.

The Last Date—Giambattista Valli shell, G-Star Raw green cargo pants, ballet flats.

Six hours in the loony bin—Robe I stole from a Four Seasons hotel in Kona (minus the tie belt—suicide risk).

Grand Canyon raft trip—Lululemon board shorts, Mion water sandals, Helly Hansen rain gear, North Face backpack, Brookstone battery-operated mini-fan, John Derian cotton sheet.

Horsey camp with Callie—AG "Kiss" jeans, Durango boots, Free People tank.

On the bus—Lucky Brand sweatpants and sweatshirt, Dansko Mary Janes.

Uniform, winter 2009—Marni dress, Marni boots, Wolford tights, Kangol hat.

And this is a remake of the song "I've Been Everywhere, Man" that I co-wrote with Beverly D'Angelo.

"I've Worn Everything, Man"

I was haulin' my ass down the busy Manhattan street
When I got to Bergdorf Goodman's with a pair of sore and
tired feet.
I'd worked my way down Madison, been to Etro and Ca-
lypso, too,
When a salesgirl walked up and she asked me, "Miss, can
I help you?"
She said, "You look to be a fashion-forward kind of girl."
I said, "Listen, I've tried on everything in this here world."

I've worn everything, man,
Shantung to gabardine, man,
Chartreuse to tangerine, man,
Chanel to L.L.Bean, man,
I've worn it I've done my thing, man,
I've worn everything . . .

Pucci, Gucci, Comme des Garçons, Betsey Johnson,
Marni, Barneys, Balenciaga, Lanvin, Prada,
Gap and Rick Owens, got my Dosa slip a-showin',
Dansko, Durango, Manolo Blahnik, it's a tonic,
Hermès, Givenchy, Demeulemeester on my keister,
Helmut Lang, Vera Wang, Donna Karan, I can wear 'em.

I've worn everything, man,
Cashmere to spandex jeans, man,
Faux fur to neoprene, man,
Fake pearls to diamond rings, man,
I've worn it I've done my thing, man,
I've worn everything.

Acknowledgments

Without the following people, this book could not have been written:

Carolyn Rosenfeld, who took dictation, did research, and held my hand.

Ken Levitan, who dared me to try.

Stokes Howell, who told the truth.

Myra Friedman, who listened.

Robin Bergland & Brad Nolen, and Liz Lambert & Amy Cook, who offered refuge.

Jack Rovner and Lisa Arzt, who cheered me on.

Grace Suh, who pulled it all together.

And to my sister.

Also deep thanks to David Mirkin; Julie Speed; Fran Christina; Lynn Spillar; Norman Sussman; Davis, Grace, and Franny McLarty; Kay Shapiro; Kay Morris; Page VanHoy; Vanessa Walters; Annie Alberino; Rosie Cusack; everyone at Vector New York; MaryAnn McCready, Kristin Braaksma, and everyone at FBMM; Mary Ellen O'Neill; David Vigliano; Deborah Triesman; Fred Bohlander and everyone at Paradigm; Living Now;

San Miguel De Allende; Kamalame Cay; Nantucket; El Cosmico; the Saint Cecilia; and the McKnight Ranch in Marfa.

To every bit of music I've ever loved, to every player who's ever moved me, to every audience member who's ever come to hear me, to every venue that has ever hosted me, my profound gratitude.

All photographs courtesy of the author with the exception of:

Permissions